La'Ron "Clown" Jones
POST TRAUMATIC STREET DISORDER
VOL. 1

La'Ron Jones

Copyright © 2024 La'Ron Jones
All rights reserved
First Edition

PAGE PUBLISHING
Conneaut Lake, PA

First originally published by Page Publishing 2024

Cover Design by Mike Ramirez and La'Ron Jones

Contact Info: Gettingout.com; Jones 081998 or 81998 ptsdvol1@gmail.com P.O. Box 24358 Omaha, NE 68124

ISBN 979-8-88960-195-1 (pbk)
ISBN 979-8-88960-208-8 (digital)

Printed in the United States of America

REVIEWS FROM INCARCERATED INDIVIDUALS

Great relatable book. This is a story of so many in the world. This book allows you to open up and have those tough conversations and believe change is possible even after real-life struggles or during incarcerations. From where La'Ron has come from to what he is doing now, he's setting positive examples for gang members on how our street struggles can inspire our youth to take a better look at themselves before it's too late. The impossible is possible!

—Chris Spears

Everything La'Ron speaks about in this book is real and authentic. Even part 1, which is based on a true story, is a relatable experience for so many, especially when we begin to look at some of these relationships that were developed early on in our lives. One thing I learned from the streets is that it doesn't show any mercy, and La'Ron does a great job of illustrating that in this book. The message that was symbolized by the dog fighting was unexpected and raw. This book is a must-read for all young gang members.

—Omar Bahati

I really appreciate La'Ron for allowing me to read this book before editing. It's real raw stories like this that must be shared with our youth. From childhood to prison this, is a very well-rounded lived experience. Change is hard, but if you are willing to make change it's possible regardless of where life takes you. This story has truly inspired me to always be willing to make that change.

—Vicente Gonzalez

This book by La'Ron Jones is an eye opener to the harsh reality of a lifestyle and life lived by so many gang members across the country. He is not glorifying the lifestyle, but narrating the raw uncut truth from a certified individual on how the streets can and will shift your mentality. Reading this book spoke to me on so many personal levels, and I highly recommend it.

—Kevin Noriega

CONTENTS

Acknowledgments vii
Preface...ix

Part 1:   Based on a True Story

    Chapter 1:   Birth of La'Ron 3
    Chapter 2:   Parentless Child..8
    Chapter 3:   Childhood Trauma 22
    Chapter 4:   Exposure 38

Part 2:   Autobiography

    Chapter 5:   The Transition..55
    Chapter 6:   The Birth of Clown 66
    Chapter 7:   Post-Traumatic Street Disorder........................78
    Chapter 8:   Warning Signs 95
    Chapter 9:   The Fear of Death 107
    Chapter 10: State of Nebraska versus Jones 120

Part 3:   From Boyhood to Manhood

    Chapter 11: The Importance of Educating Yourself
                   while Incarcerated 137

Questions for Book Club 153

ACKNOWLEDGMENTS

First and foremost, all praise goes to God.

My grandmother, the first queen of my universe, Betty Spencer: Oftentimes, I have been characterized as different, humble, respectful, and strong-minded. It's because of you that when I'm faced with adversity, I have such a strong core foundation to stand on.

My mother, the second queen of my universe, Debbie Spencer: Just thinking about your strength brings tears of joy to my eyes. In my mind, you were the first female hustler I ever met. Our journey has been a rocky one, but it's one where we have always been transparent with each other. I acknowledge for a woman it isn't easy trying to raise a man, but I thank you for giving me the space to discover myself. Love you!

My siblings—Pra'Shae, La'Che, Arrionna, and Charles: Your safety and well-being has always been a priority of mine. I wish nothing but the best for you all.

My fallen soldiers/associates—OG Monie, OG C'ion, OG Mezzo, Blue, Savo, NoNo, Maxxo, E-Bo, Penny, Fatts, Big Rome, Cell-G: Only you'll would know. Is there a heaven for a gangster?

Special thanks to all my supporters that have been holding me down and checking up on me at the lowest point in my life. Having your support has helped me in more ways than you may ever imagine. You all are in my prayers, and I can't wait till we meet again on the other side of these vertical walls.

My son, Kingzton Jones: "Our deepest fear is not that we are inadequate. Our deepest fear is that we are powerful beyond measure. It is our light, not our darkness, that frightens us most. We ask ourselves, 'Who am I to be brilliant, gorgeous, talented, and famous?' Actually, who are you not to be? You are a child of God. Your playing

Acknowledgments

small does not serve the world. There is nothing enlightened about shrinking so that people won't feel insecure around you. We were born to make manifest the glory of God that is within us. It's not just in some of us; it's in all of us. And when we let our own light shine, we unconsciously give other people permission to do the same. As we are liberated from our own fears, our presence automatically liberates others" (Nelson Mandela).

PREFACE

This book you are about to read would make it seem as if you were in the room talking with me face-to-face. Unfortunately, many young men and women will end up in prison, and as my dear friend Avery Tyler Sr. would say, "There is a vicious cycle that few speak about that occurs in impoverished communities where young women and men are being sentenced to decades of incarceration with no opportunity to heal the very community that we've harmed." Ultimately, this book is a very small fraction of the debt I owe to my community, and that's why a fraction of the proceeds from this book will go back to surrounding communities.

The first part of this book is based on a true story of my lived experience, and there are two reasons why I decided to design this book that way.

One, for many of us there's so much we don't remember about our childhood, which is the case for me. I wanted to create a narrative around some of the stories I remembered and heard about growing up that impacted my life.

Two, from my experience of being young once and also from being around youths, I see that most of them would much rather read hood novels. From the book cover to the language, this is my strategic way to catch the young readers' attention. The first part of this book covers various of childhood experiences, from abandonment issues, identity issues, growing up without parent(s), school experiences, friendships, searching for acceptance, bullying, and so forth. But one of the main focuses is on the hypocritical advice we are fed by the storytellers/elders around us that oftentimes distort our worldview.

Preface

The second part of this book is all facts—the autobiography. For those who grew up living a life of illegal activities I think we can all agree that there was a starting point, which often exists between middle school and high school. As my dear friend Terence Johnson would say, "No one was born to live a life of committing crimes; something happened along the way." Gang members are often politicized to be the worse of the worse. Conversations about lowering the crime rates and getting guns off the streets has had the power to put so many of our city officials in office, which in turn opens the door for us to get harsh lengthy prison sentences.

The third part of this book is about my paradigm shift from boyhood to manhood with book club questions included. As I began to take on the task of educating myself, I earned my high school diploma and also participated in other programs/classes that had a major impact in my life—to name a few: Prison Fellowship Academy, Community Justice Center Victim Impact Class, *The 7 Habits of Highly Effective People, Intentional Peer Support,* **and Defy Ventures (now known as Rise).** The fact remains that one way to slow down the cycle is by bringing awareness to the problems and allow our at-risk youths/gang members to see a reflection of *what's possible* when it relates to respected ex-gang-members who have changed their life. No matter what some in society may think gang members are capable of change. Rather we allow incarcerated individuals to visit or live at youth facilities or incarcerated individuals to visit alternative schools. We must remind ourselves that "You can't be what you can't see." And for all of our at-risk youth/young gang members, they may have never had anyone who shared their street experience and saw them change into a better person. This in turn could help us solve a bigger problem. When we began to search for life's changing answers, one of the main questions should be, how do we transform trauma into emotional intelligence? And part of that answer from my worldview is those who were once a part of the problem must be a part of the solution. We must continue to advocate to create a space where it's socially acceptable for gang members to share their experience with our at-risk youths/gang members with the message that it's okay to step away from the gang life in order to step into your womanhood or manhood. Because just how gang members arrive at this moment of searching for acceptance, respect, and love outside of their households, to living a life of crime, there's a street image that's projected from negative role models that we tend to imitate in order to gain that same level of acceptance, respect, and love. This phase in our life causes us to lose sight of our own identity.

But on the flip side, I also believe that all gang members arrive at a point where we are well aware that something in our lives need to change for the better. We often realize that we have stepped away from some of those core values we learned as kids, then pick up on the codes of the streets. During this process we struggle with how to step into this new being we wish to create or get back to, struggling to understand the true meaning of change and what that should look like for us. I hope this book can be the start of you looking at yourself objectively and understanding the change you want for yourself is a process, but it's a process that's very achievable with the proper self, social, emotional, and community awareness. With this reflection, you can learn to mitigate or stop certain negative patterns. You can work to transform the negative and weak aspects of your character into actual strengths.

*Outside of my father committing suicide and me beating up Milton's bully, all crimes in part 1 of this book are false.

PART 1

Based on a True Story

CHAPTER 1

Birth of La'Ron

March 27, 1990, 3:37 a.m. It was a dark and rainy morning in Dumas, Arkansas. The clouds were thick, and over the light thunder and raindrops, the voice of the thirteen-year-old girl, Debbie Spencer, screamed out repeatedly, "Take me to the hospital! Please, I'm in pain!"

Her mother, Betty Spencer, ran into the room and noticed the liquid dripping from her young daughter's legs. "Calm down, child. Our ride is on the way," said Ms. Spencer.

"Mom, why does it hurt so bad?" asked Debbie.

"Just relax, child. Our ride should be pulling up any minute. Just stay calm."

Debbie Spencer was a beautiful dark-skinned young lady. If there were ever a role for a beautiful young African princess, the job would be hers. She was a disobedient child who often played hooky from school and ran around the neighborhood with older boys. Anybody who knew Debbie would say she had great potential. Betty was looking into Debbie eye's and realizing that her daughter's potential was slowly fading away.

Betty was a very strong-minded woman. She had seven kids: Anthony, Jerry, Duke, David, Greg, Shanta, and Debbie. She held a steady job for years at the local Cotton Gin. On the weekends, she was a downhome blues–type of lady who could cut a rug. You could often spot her in the juke joint two-stepping and drinking hard liquor. Overall Betty was truly a Black queen in her own right. She kept a roof over her kids' head, dinner was cooked every night, and if not, there was always something to eat in the refrigerator. She was known for keeping a boyfriend around the house with a good job, and when it was time to pay the bills, she didn't hesitate to dig in his pockets. Everyone in the neighborhood respected her word. Everyone in the neighborhood also knew she did a prison bid for poisoning her ex-husband after being beaten one too many times.

"Beep! Beep! Let's go, child! Your aunt Dessa is outside to pick us up!" As they drove off to the hospital, Betty was still in disbelief that her thirteen-year-old daughter was about to have a baby. Betty just had Shanta who was three years old, and now she would have her first grandchild. Even though Betty felt great about becoming a grandmother, she couldn't help but to feel guilt with the fact that her baby was having a baby.

As Betty gazed out the window while her sister Dessa controlled the wheel at a high rate of speed, Debbie couldn't help but to notice that her mom was stuck staring off into space. "What are you thinking about, Mom?" she asked.

"I'm just not sure how things are going to work out with you being a thirteen-year-old parent," she said.

"Well, maybe you should just have the baby since you are so worried about it," Debbie exclaimed.

"Nah, that is your responsibility. If you were woman enough to lay down and make a baby, you should be woman enough to take care of it," her mother added.

"Yeah, yeah, yeah…we'll see about that," Debbie said, rolling her eyes.

"What do you mean, we'll see about that?" Betty asked.

"I don't know, Mom. I'm not so sure about being a parent. I'm already having a hard time in school. I depend on you for food, housing, and clothes. I'm too young for my own place. I'm just not ready."

"Well, you better get ready, young lady. If you didn't hide your pregnancy for all those months, we could have made a decision on you getting an abortion," Betty said, rolling her eyes.

"And live with that memory forever? That would have hurt me more, taking a baby's life," Debbie said with a frown on her young face.

"Your body, your choice!" said Betty.

Squeak.

"Bonding time is over, ladies, we are here," said Dessa.

As they rushed through the emergency doors, a doctor quickly came to their aid with a wheelchair. As Debbie got closer and closer to the room, she felt as if her heart was about to jump out her chest. She groaned in pain as she was soaking in sweat, nervously thinking about how much pain she was about to endure pushing a baby out her small frame.

The wait alone was driving Debbie crazy. After what seemed like hours of waiting and preparation, a doctor yelled, "It's time!"

"Push, push, push!" was all you heard in the room as the young Debbie screamed out in pain. "On the count of three, give it all you got. One, two…three!"

"Aw!" Debbie screamed. *Pfft*, she farted.

"Okay! Good job, Debbie! The head is out, but we have one problem. The umbilical is wrapped around the baby's neck."

"Is my baby going to be okay?" asked Debbie.

"Yes, he will be fine! It will take a few seconds of shifting the baby around, but this won't be a major problem. Okay, I got it. It's all downhill from here, especially once we're past the shoulders."

"Just pull it out!" Debbie screamed. Betty couldn't help but to laugh at the thought of relating to her daughter's pain. As Debbie gripped her hand tighter and tighter to her mother's hand, she patiently waited as the doctors worked on getting the baby out. After what seem like hours of pushing and screaming, finally the baby boy had arrived. Debbie's first thought while looking at her son was "What a painful blessing!"

"It's a boy," the doctor said, smiling sarcastically. "What are you going to name him?"

"La'Ron. La'Ron Mar'Quis Jones," Debbie said.

Betty looked at her daughter with confusion. She recalled the father's name was Timothy Jackson, but she kept her mouth shut.

Birth of La'Ron

She knew when they got home, they would have a conversation about what she just heard. *There is always something with this girl,* Betty thought to herself.

As the doctors cleaned up the mess and took La'Ron to do all his check-ups, Betty congratulated her daughter. "I never want you to go through that pain again!" Debbie said as they all bust out laughing. "Well, I'm about to leave. I got to get ready for work. I'll be back when I get off tomorrow. If you need anything before then, don't hesitate to call my job. One more thing before I go, I want you to know that I love you, and believe that you are going to be a great mother. There is nothing in this world that you cannot do or be, you just have to believe in yourself."

"Mom, the problem is, I'm not sure what to believe. I'm not sure what to do."

"Have faith, child. No pain, no gain!"

Betty left the room with those words looming in the air.

When Betty got off work the next day, her body wouldn't allow her to make the trip to the hospital. Once she got home and checked her answering machine, to her surprise, Debbie didn't call home—not one time. The worrying was starting to kick in, but she told herself maybe her daughter was taking the day to rest. The next day, while Betty was at work, the worrying became more intense, and her boss, James, was starting to notice her lack of energy. As she picked the visible seeds and stems from the cotton before running it through the machine, her name blasted over the intercom. "Betty Spencer, please report to the main office." As she walked toward the office, she expected the worst. She knew anytime someone's name was called over the loudspeaker that was usually not a good thing. Even though she had been at the job for almost seventeen years, on and off, she had the mindset that nothing was promised.

"Yes, James?"

"Come in! Shut the door behind you, please. How is everything going, Betty? The last week or so you haven't been showing much initiative. You're communicating less. Are you okay?"

"Well, James, my thirteen-year-old daughter just had a baby boy. She had complications with the birth; the umbilical cord was wrapped around the baby's neck, and he also came out premature. And my daughter is talking like she isn't sure about being a parent and even hinted that she didn't want the baby. On top of all that, I got a three-year-old baby that I'm raising."

"Betty, one thing that I respect about you is that you are a strong-minded woman and very respectful. I'm sure within due time you will figure out a way to put your family in the best position possible. As you know, Connie will be retiring in less than three days. You've been here longer than anybody, and I would like for you to be our new floor supervisor."

"What? Are you serious? I would love that. It would be such a huge blessing for my family."

"Okay, great. I got to go over your file and get it to my secretary so she can put you in for a raise next month. Until then, get back to work. The longer you sit in my office, the more production slows down."

"Okay, thank you so much for the opportunity." With that being said, she walked out the office with her head held high and a whole new energy. She was proud to be recognized for all the years of putting in hard work and even more proud to be able to set the tone for Black women in the workplace in the small town of Dumas, Arkansas. Having a Black female supervisor of any sort was historically rare, and Betty Spencer was proud that she had just broken a barrier for so many women in her community.

REVIEW BOOK CLUB QUESTIONS.

CHAPTER 2

Parentless Child

Ring, ring, ring. "Thank you for calling James's Cotton Gin. This is Engrasha speaking. How may I help you?"

"Yes, Engrasha, this is Dr. Buggs at the Dumas Hospital. I would like to know if Betty Spencer is in. It is very important that I speak with her."

"Yes, one moment, Doctor."

"Betty Spencer! Please report to the main office!" As Betty heard the call, all kinds of negative thoughts were running through her head. She replayed the conversation that she and James had and how he had to go through her file.

"Yes, James?"

"You have a call from a doctor on the line. If you'd like, you can use the phone in here so you don't have to talk around the office staff."

She thought to herself, *This nosy man just wants to eavesdrop on my conversation.* "Hello, this is Betty speaking."

"Yes, Ms. Spencer, this is Dr. Buggs speaking. I apologize for calling you at your job, but I'm very concerned about Debbie. I went to her room to let her know that she and La'Ron could leave the hospital, and to my surprise, she wasn't there. I waited an hour or so and then went back, but she still wasn't there."

"I get off in thirty minutes, Dr. Buggs, and I'll come straight there. I really do appreciate you giving me a call."

When Betty arrived at the hospital, all she could think about was the conversation she and Debbie had in the car about how she wasn't ready to be a parent. "What am I going to do? How can I finesse the doctor into allowing me to take La'Ron without Debbie? Maybe I'll fake the call." Betty waited patiently as the phone rang to her sister Dessa's house.

"Hello! Hey, I need a favor."

"What now?"

"I'm here at the hospital, and to my surprise, it seems as if Debbie has left and abandoned her baby. Whatever the case may be, I got to play it safe. I can't give my first grandchild up and allow the state to take him. I'm going to tell the doctor that Debbie is at home hurting, stressing, and resting and that she gave me consent to come get La'Ron. The thing is he might call my house to get a verbal consent. I know it will take you about seven minutes to get to my house. Can you please get there? One of the boys will let you in."

"Okay, sis. I got you. Keep your fingers crossed that Debbie pops up."

Betty's plan worked out perfectly. About three and a half months went by, and she only heard from Debbie once. When she did speak with her daughter, Debbie threatened to take the baby if she didn't get $250 for a bus fare to Kansas so she could be with her dad's side of the family. After replaying numerous of conversations that she and her daughter had about the responsibility around being a young mother, Betty knew it would be in her and La'Ron's best interest if she just gave Debbie the money. Betty gave her the money and didn't hear anything from her daughter after that. I guess one would say that she sold her son.

Around the fifth month, Betty decided to get in touch with the boy's father. She knew where his family stayed but decided to call first before she just stops by. She grabbed the phonebook and searched under Jackson and in no time found who she was looking for. After a moment of pondering on whether she should call or not, she knew that making this decision wasn't about her feelings but more about La'Ron and Timothy having the right to build a relationship with each other.

Parentless Child

Timothy's mom, Essie Jackson, was a strong Southern woman who was the backbone for Dumas's biggest hustler, Toney Jackson. They owned a large piece of land with three houses on the lot, which included a club or, as the old folks would say, a juke joint that operated Thursday night through early Sunday morning. Some would say that her husband, Toney, was the biggest heroin dealer in the small town even though there is no record of him ever getting caught. After Toney died and left Essie with four kids, she ended up turning her life around, left the after-hours business and devoted her life to God.

Ring, ring, ring.

"Hello! This is Essie speaking."

"Hello! My name is Betty Spencer and I have something very important that I would like to speak with you about. I would like to speak with you and your son Timothy in person."

"May I ask what about?"

"Well, let me start by saying that I truly apologize for taking so long to contact y'all, but it is my understanding that Timothy is the father of my five-month-old grandson."

"What's the boy's name?"

"La'Ron Mar'Quis Jones. I'll explain the Jones part later."

"Well, do you know that Timothy is only fifteen?"

"Yes, and my daughter Debbie was thirteen when she birthed La'Ron."

"Kids these days! Well, Timothy is outside cutting the grass. He'll be in soon. I have some fried chicken, brown beans, biscuits, white rice, and gravy that I'm preparing, so if you like, you and La'Ron can stop by and have a bite to eat with us. You know where I live?"

"Yes, I know where you live. I will be there in less than an hour."

Timothy was a very smart young man. He was light-skinned stocky built soft-spoken and the youngest of Essie's four kids. He was super-creative and the neighborhood's go-to guy for yard work, house work, and most things in between. Everyone knew if you wanted something done fast, and at a reasonable price, you went to Timothy. He was a hustler like his dad. As he stepped into the house, his stomach started rumbling as soon as he caught a whiff of what was cooking.

"Hey, Mama Essie, why are you moving so fast?"

"We are expecting some visitors."

"Is it those church people again?"

"Ha ha! No, Timothy. I got a call from Betty Spencer, Debbie Spencer's mom, and she said that her five-month-old grandson is your son."

Timothy scratched his head. "Well, Mom, if he's five months old, then I will say that the timeline adds up. Debbie and I were together for a short period of time, but the strange thing is that I haven't heard from her in months."

"She never told you that she might be pregnant?"

"Well, yeah. But yeah, I never took her seriously or put too much thought behind it, especially after not hearing from her."

"Well, son, this is a small town and I understand that we live a small town away. If you knew this information and didn't want to tell me, the least you could have done was hopped on your bike and check to see if the young lady was okay. I'm surprised you kept something this important from me; this is not like you, Timothy. Well, go get yourself cleaned up. They should be here any minute." As the knock echoed from the door, Timothy began to sweat. His mind was racing, just thinking about the responsibility that comes with being a father. *Here goes nothing,* he thought to himself.

"Hello! Well, I'm guessing that you are Timothy?" Betty said.

"Hello, Ms. Spencer. Yes, I'm Timothy, and that must be La'Ron your holding?"

"Yes, it is."

Timothy reached to pull the blanket to reveal the baby's face, and at first sight, he couldn't deny the fact that the baby looked like a dark-skinned version of himself and his dad.

Essie came out to greet Betty and the baby. "Ain't no denying this one, Timothy. Look at that nose," she said, smiling.

As they ate dinner, Betty explained everything to them and what took place with La'Ron's birth, the complications, and also how Debbie moved to Kansas to be with her dad side of the family. She explained her struggles of having a three-year-old baby at home and having to raise La'Ron at the same time. In that moment, Timothy knew he needed to step up to the plate in a major way. He heard the pain in Betty's voice, and it reminded him of some of the conversations he and his dad had about being a man and taking care of responsibilities. Timothy went from having a dad to being a fatherless child, and above all else, he knew he didn't want La'Ron growing up experiencing those same feelings he felt.

"Well, Betty, I'm going to do everything in my power to help you with La'Ron. Timothy, you got anything to say?" said Essie.

"Yes, Ms. Spencer. My father has always played a major role in my life, so I understand how important it is for me to be in La'Ron's life and be a great example for him on what a man should be like. As you know, there is not much work in this town, but I do well doing small jobs around the community, especially during the summer. Tomorrow, if it is okay with my mom, I'm going to take the day off from school so I can go to the other side of the tracks and try to find a few new gigs."

"Timothy, I have no doubt you're going to be a great dad. On another note, I do think it is time for me and La'Ron to head out. If it is okay with Mrs. Jackson, I will start dropping La'Ron off every weekend so y'all can spend time with him as well." Betty and La'Ron looked at Mrs. Jackson at the same time, noticing that she had been quiet since they sat at the lunch table.

"Excuse me," Betty said, snapping Essie out her quietness, "I would love to have La'Ron here. I will be looking forward to seeing La'Ron every weekend, and so will Timothy. Let me fix you a plate to go. Timothy, take La'Ron to the car while we're wrapping up this food. Another thing, Betty. Is it okay if we take La'Ron to church with us?"

"Of course, Essie!"

As Timothy was walking to the car with his son, La'Ron finally woke up. "Hey, son, I'm going to work on getting that last name changed. I want you to know I'm not sure how to be a father and I know you are not clear on how to be a son," he said, smiling, "but I'm going to do my best to provide for you in every way possible. I cannot wait for you to get older so I can teach you everything my dad taught me. I guess there's the positive to both of us being young. I'll be thirty when you turn fifteen, so I'm sure I'll still be able to keep up with you." Timothy reached out his index finger, and La'Ron grabbed it with a full grip. "I love you, kiddo," Timothy said, looking at La'Ron in his eyes. He smiled at Timothy for the first time. As he tucked him in and sat there looking at his latest creation, the baby slowly nodded back off to sleep. "Dream big!"

The next day, Timothy woke up thinking about ways to become a great father and how he could put himself in position to help Betty provide for his son. When it came to the yard work he was doing around the neighborhood, he was only making money on his side of town and had everything on the north side except for the Coner boys' properties because before his dad died he warned him to stay away from that crowd. Deep down inside, he knew he was missing out on a lot of money by not doing business with the crew, but he thought to himself there would be no harm done by doing yard work on a few of their properties, and he knew just the guy that could put him in position.

A guy from school named Gat Green. Gat was the second in command for the Vill Side Boyz and even approached Timothy about giving him a job, but Timothy declined. One day, Timothy ran across a case full of guns at an abandoned house where he was mowing the lawn. He knew they could only belong to one person, so he approached Gat and advised him to move the guns. Timothy told Gat before doing the lawn the landlord spoke to him about some people moving into the house soon, so that meant if he didn't go get the guns in time, then someone else would have most likely discovered them. Gat greatly appreciated Timothy giving him this information, and ever since then, he had the utmost respect for Timothy and gave him the green light, which means he never got robbed or shook down by the Vill Side Boyz. Regardless of all that, Timothy knew this was going to be a hard conversation to have with Gat. He knew Gat was super-paranoid, and asking him to work on some of his personal properties may seem suspicious to Gat and mess up their agreement.

Timothy also knew that if outsiders or police saw him doing these properties, they would associate him as being a part of the gang.

The following day Timothy saw Gat and made his move. "Yo, Gat! Can I holla at you for a minute?"

"Yeah, what's up?"

"I don't mean to bother you with my personal problems, but I just found out I got a son and I'm looking to expand my hustle."

"Aww, man. Pretty boy Tim is ready to get into the dope game."

"Nah, man. It ain't nothing like that. You know my style. I only do honest-man work. None of that poison."

"Poison? Yeah okay, Timothy. From what I hear, you need to thank your dad and his old partner, El-Roy, for that. They're the ones who introduced the southern part of this state to the drug trade, but that's neither here nor there. I have to get the green light from my boss, Big Vill. I'll meet you at the park at 7:00 p.m. You know, One Shot might not be so happy to hear you are trying to step on his toes."

"Look, Gat, stepping on toes is what I don't do. The truth is I'm better at the line of work I and One Shot do, and I have better equipment. Plus, he's been loyal to you for years. I see him all the time working and grinding hard. Give him a promotion so there won't be any bad blood."

"Yeah, that's a good idea. I'll holla at Big Vill. Just make sure you be at the park on time tonight." As Timothy turned to walk off, Gat called his name. "Yo, Timothy! Who is the lucky lady?"

"Debbie Spencer."

"Debbie Spencer? I haven't seen her in forever. Don't let me find out you got her locked in your shed so I can't get to her," Gat said, smiling.

"Haha, you got jokes! Yeah, it's been a minute since I saw her as well. She lives in Kansas now. She left the baby with her mom."

"Well, I wish you the best of luck, pretty boy Tim."

Timothy had been sitting in the park for twenty minutes when Gat and One Shot pulled up on their dirt bikes. "What's good, Timothy? I got a deal for you. You can do all the maintenance on all the properties except the main house and two of the stash houses. As you know, we have a dog kennel connected to the hog farm on the back street where we breed dogs with OG D-Low and El-Roy. That spot has to be done every day, plus feeding the dogs, spraying them down, and giving them water, but you are never to enter the slaughterhouse. Not one inch of that land. If you do so, you will be fired immediately. Altogether, you will be doing ten properties for us at $100 each, $1,000 a month. Of course, you have better equipment than One Shot, but you don't have a truck so we are throwing one in as a part of the deal too. The truck will cost you $2,000. Either you can pay for it out of your pocket or receive $500 a month for the next four months to work the two grand off. What you think?"

"A thousand a month is a little light, Gat. I have to cut nine yards a week on top of doing maintenance if anything goes wrong. I have to do the dog kennel every day. After buying gas my profit might only be five or six hundred dollars, which I have to turn around and give you for the truck. Boy, boy, boy, I see why Big Vill made you his righthand man. I guess the streets wasn't lying when they said you played for keeps. Gat, I have an offer for you. I will give you a $1,000 up front now for the truck but only if we sign the title over tonight and you don't start taking the $500 till my third month."

"Um, then the title is yours."

"Then the deal is done. One Shot will meet you tomorrow to show you all the locations. And, Timothy? I don't think I have to tell you, but I really do play for keeps. With that being said, don't ever touch or take anything that don't belong to you and don't ever speak to anyone about our locations or what you see. Not even your mom."

"Gat, you know I know better than that. I'm out, One Shot. I will catch up with you as soon school ends tomorrow."

As they sat watching Timothy walk away, One Shot was furious. "Damn, Gat, you'll be paying that brother more money per property than me. I was only getting $80 a location."

"Yeah, One Shot, but you also sell drugs and he doesn't. Plus, I like him; that boy is a true hustler. Money is going to be the death of that kid. You watch, One Shot."

"I agree, that sounds about right, Gat. Money will be the death of that kid."

Timothy was excited. He knew what this move meant for his business and overall the support he would be able to provide for La'Ron. He understood how the whole city operated. He knew Big Vill and Gat controlled the north side, mainly dealing crack cocaine and guns. Detondrick controlled the crew on the east side, the East Side Boyz, mainly dealing marijuana and racing cars. El-Roy, Foot, and D-Low controlled the largest part of the town, which was the west, mainly dealing heroin and livestock. Downtown and the south was where the Whites operated. It was also where all the local businesses and stores was located.

Timothy walked home at a high rate of speed. He couldn't wait to tell his mom about his new jobs. As he stuck the key in the door, he heard the TV playing, which meant Mama Essie was still awake.

"Hey, Mom."

"Hi, baby. How was your day?"

"It was great. I ended up landing a new job that pays $1,000 a month."

"That's awesome! What will you be doing?"

"Before you interrupt or get worried, just hear me out. I will be doing yard work on Big Vill properties, but only the ones he rent out," Timothy said lying, with the hopes to ease his mom's worries. "Mom, I'm a father now and I'm trying to put myself in the best position to be a great father."

"I can understand that, Timothy. I trust you to make the right decisions! I know that one guy, One Sack, One Fat, One Shot, or whatever his name is has been doing yard work for them as well. How does he feel about that?"

"Lol! It's One Shot, Mom. He is on board. Gat gave him a promotion, and he's even going to sell me a truck for two grand."

"I knew taking you to get your learner's permit would come in handy sooner than you thought."

"You're not slick, Mom. You did that so I could drive you to church. Plus, there are four police officers in this whole town, and they know who I am and what I do, so I think I would have been okay without it," Timothy said, smiling.

"Okay, son. Just be careful. You know One Shot's reputation. It seems like the people who deal with him comes up missing a lot. I'm surprise the police haven't indicted him yet."

"That's what they say. Once again, I will have nothing to do with him after tomorrow."

"Okay, I trust what you say. I'm going to sleep. Love you, baby."

"Love you too, Mom."

Timothy woke up to the sound of a dirt bike engine; he knew it had to be One Shot. He looked out his window, and to no surprise, that's who it was. "Let me get dressed, then I'll be right out."

"What's up, One Shot?" Timothy said.

"I figured it would be best if we skip the first half of school today so I can show you these locations, and also head to the DMV to get the title switched over."

After checking out all the properties, they finally arrived at the DMV. "Man, One Shot. It took you all day."

"I guess that means I did a good job of showing you the properties and giving you the game."

"You did all right. I know one thing is for sure. It could have been more showing and less talking." They both busted out laughing. One Shot replied, "Shut up, lame!" and they laughed even harder.

They approached the counter at the DMV when the clerk greeted them asking, "How may I help you, gentlemen, today?" After stating their purpose, she handed them some paperwork to fill out and charged them $77 for processing the paperwork. "How are you paying today?"

"Cash! "Timothy said after pulling out a bankroll of money. One Shot's eyes lit up at the sight of the wad of money.

After they left the DMV with the change made, One Shot couldn't help but ask Timothy how he had been doing so well for himself.

"Man, One Shot, don't be pocket watching. But to answer your question, it's all about consistency and money management. I'm always on time to work, and I don't buy what I want. I buy what I need."

"Pocket watching, come on! You know I wouldn't dare touch you. Your dad is a street legend in this town, and El-Roy would go crazy if I did anything to you."

"I and El-Roy don't even talk."

"Trust me, that is for your own safety. Don't think he don't got eyes on you. But let's change the subject. I got a couple guys coming in from different parts of Arkansas in a few weeks. Mostly a handful of contract killers who just love the look and smell of blood. I host this game once a year called Russian Roulette. I usually do two games, six guys, but one of the players was just found dead. Do you want in?"

"How does the game work?"

"The prize is ten grand. You will be blindfolded. You put one bullet in the gun, spin the barrel, and then pull the trigger. You have to put $1,000 up front. After the first person is dead, the remaining two players have the option to split the pot 30-70. For you, I'll do a solid, I'll let you get in the game for $700 only if we agree that once you pass the first round, you take the 30 split, which will be 3 grand, minus your $700 you put in, so that will be $2,300 in profit."

Timothy couldn't help but to think how helpful having the extra money would be. He would be able to pay off the truck and have an extra $300 to spend on oil and gas.

"One Shot, we both know there is no guarantee that I will make it through the second round."

"Let me handle that part. I'll rig the game to make sure that you will be the third person taking the shot, but that's as far as I can take it."

"Okay, One Shot, I'm in."

"Coo! Let me get that $700 right now," One Shot said with a devilish grin on his face.

The weeks was going well for Timothy. He worked till 8:00 p.m. on school days, and on the weekends, he got a 7:00 a.m. start and would be finished by 5:00 p.m. At the end of the day he always made sure to make time to stop by Betty's house to spend time with La'Ron, and on the weekends he couldn't wait to get off work so he could end his night with his son sleeping next to his side. Timothy finally had it all together; life was great!

A little over three weeks had passed when Timothy finally got the call from One Shot. "It's time, Timothy! You know where to be, 7:00 p.m. sharp." Timothy was nervous, but he knew that this was not the time to freeze up now. Overall, he relied on One Shot's word about rigging the game, and for him that was good enough to take the gamble.

Timothy had a few hours to spare, so he decided to go spend time with La'Ron. Luckily when he got there La'Ron was woke and full of energy. Timothy sat on the floor and played with his son for over an hour, but time went by so fast it seemed like it had only been a few minutes. As he prepared to leave, he told Betty that he would be back after work tomorrow, then gazed at his five-month-old baby boy in the eyes and said goodbye. Betty interrupted their gaze. "Never tell your son goodbye. Bye means forever. Tell him that you will see him later."

Timothy replied, "You're right! I never thought about it that way. I'll see you both later," Timothy said, smiling.

Timothy arrived near a building where he fed and cleaned the dogs. He had never been inside, but he knew this was the place One Shot had told him to be. There were two guys standing next to a locked gate. At the sight of Timothy's truck, the gate was unchained and open. Once he saw the faded red barn and the huge sign that read "Slaughterhouse," his heart started to race. As he slowly walked through the front door, he was surprised by the cleanliness of the building. As they walked toward the back of the barn Timothy noticed that most of the rooms were boxed in by plexiglass, and he saw many different types of animals hanging on hooks as he passed by. They arrived at two sliding doors at the back of the building, which led to a large fridge storing milk. As the strange man reached and grabbed one of the milks it pulled as a lever, which revealed a hidden narrow passage that led to the basement. At the sight of the crowd, Timothy took a deep breath and told himself, "It's time!"

One Shot lit up once he saw Timothy come through the narrow door. "Just the man we was waiting on. Let's get this show started."

First up. *Click*. Second up. *Click*. Third up. *Boom.* Timothy's brain was now scattered all over the floor and wall from the burst of the 44 magnum. In that moment, One Shot knew that his life was over. He knew this meant that he would have to answer to El-Roy and Big Vill.

"What's the odds!" One Shot said to himself. "What's the odds!" After every game, One Shot did his usual. He paid the crew, the winner(s), then took the body to the hogs to be disposed. He would then meet with D-Low to pay him for using the property. To his surprise, when he entered the room, El-Roy and Big Vill had been there waiting on him to arrive. There was no doubt in his mind that this was a terrible sign.

"El-Roy, Big Vill, how y'all doing?" One Shot said.

"All is well," Big Vill replied. "How was your night?"

"It was good. Due to all the spectators that came to watch, I ended up with $3,000 more than I made last year. The last two guys didn't split the money. They went to the end, so that was amazing."

El-Roy stood up. "Enough of the small talk. What about Timothy?"

"Well—"

El-Roy interrupted his thought. "You know, kid, this makes me want to personally cut your feet and hands off and throw you into the hog pen myself, but since you're under Big Vill's leadership, it's his responsibility to punish you how he sees fit."

El-Roy sat down, and Big Vill stood up.

"One Shot, you have disappointed me and the Vill Side organization. For years, we've allowed you to run your business at a small cost and also under the specific order not to allow any guys from Dumas to participate. I'm not sure what to do with you. I have two ideas running through my mind. Since I respect you enough as a man, I'm going to let you choose. The first option is to do exactly what El-Roy suggested. The second option is sparing your life, but you must go tell Essie Jackson everything that happened to her son, everything!"

"Okay, Big Vill. I will do just that."

"Good. Gat is on the way to take you over there now."

"Now?"

"Yeah, now!" Big Vill said while waving for Gat to come in. One Shot walked out with his head down, regretting what happened to Timothy. Big Vill called Gat over to his table to give him final orders. "Gat, after he tells Essie Jackson what happened, I want you to shoot him up with heroin, and I don't never want to hear about One Shot making another dollar off any organization in this state."

El-Roy wasn't satisfied. Even though he allowed every man in the nearby towns to run their own crew, he was the boss of all bosses. If he called a shot, it was final and never questioned. El-Roy stood up. "D-Low I want you to go with Gat. Fill up a needle and inject One Shot with a shot of the purest heroin we got. Do this every day for the next two weeks, then cut him loose." El-Roy walked out without anyone questioning a word he said.

Gat couldn't help but to think about the last conversation he had with his righthand man, One Shot, about Timothy and how money was going to be the death of Timothy. "Another parentless child," Gat said out loud while shaking his head in total disbelief. "Another parentless child!"

REVIEW BOOK CLUB QUESTIONS.

CHAPTER 3

Childhood Trauma

Five years later

"La'Ron, wake up! It's time to get ready for school!" Betty yelled.

"I'm woke, Grandma," replied La'Ron.

"Get your butt up and get dressed. The bus will be here in less than thirty minutes."

"Where are my clothes, Grandma?"

"If you was woke, you would see that they are sitting right there on your dresser. I ironed them last night."

"You're the best, Grandma!"

"Best! Best get your butt up out my house and go to school. Are you nervous for the first day?"

"Nah, I'm not nervous. I'm ready to go meet some new friends."

"Okay, La'Ron! Please just keep in mind, you're not going to school only to meet new friends. You are going to learn so you can grow up to be very smart and become a wealthy man."

"Yeah, Grandma, and I will be able to buy you everything in the whole world!"

Betty laughed and replied, "Yeah, I can't wait for that day to come."

* * * * *

"Hello, class, my name is Mrs. K Canada. Today, everyone will come to the front of the class to introduce themselves, and after that, I would like for y'all to pair up with another student that you have something in common with. We are going to go in alphabetical order by last name, from A to Z. We have ten boys and eleven girls. I want the boys to pair with boys and girls to pair with girls, and one of you lucky ladies will pair with me."

After the introduction process was over, it was time to pair up. La'Ron had spotted a kid across the room who caught his attention.

"Hey, my name is La'Ron Jones. What's your name?"

"My name is Milton Butler."

"Hey, Milton. I see we have on the same Nike shoes, so would you like to pair up?"

"My Nikes are black and yours are white, do you think that matters?"

"I don't think that matters, Milton."

After the pairing was done and each pair explained why they paired up with each other, Mrs. Canada quickly took a liking to La'Ron and Milton. She could tell that La'Ron was a very smart kid. After spending more time with them, she understood that the two boys had more in common than they had thought. Milton was also living a life without parents. Both of his parents were living separate lives in Omaha, Nebraska. Milton lived with his uncle, who was a good hard-working Southern man, who went to work six days a week. He was very strict when it came to raising Milton.

Milton was a very quiet kid, but when he spoke, he never failed to ask a million questions. He was a couple months older than La'Ron but smaller. He had brown skin and always kept a nice haircut with the 360 waves. He was always well-dressed, but there wasn't a day that went by that he didn't come to school smelling like moth balls.

In no time, La'Ron and Milton became best friends, and as the years went by it became impossible to spot one without the other. They developed a saying together: "We all we got." People would notice that they were inseparable.

Childhood Trauma

Years later

"Man, Milton, I'm glad today is the last day of school."

"Yeah, me too. What do you have planned for the summer? As you know, I been talking to my mom on and off. Come to find out I have two little sisters. My mom's supposed to come down this summer so we can meet each other."

"Are you nervous, La'Ron?"

"Yeah, a little. I have only seen her through pictures."

"When they leave, are you going to go back with them?"

"I'm not sure if my grandma will let me, and honestly, I don't think I want to live with her."

"Why not?"

"Stop asking a million questions, Milton. What do you got planned for the summer?"

"I don't know. My uncle probably is going to have me in church as much as possible. Other than that, my plans are the usual: basketball at the fish house, football on whatever field you decide to get beat on…I'm hanging with you!"

La'Ron noticed that Milton was quiet and looking down at the ground as if he had something weighing on his mind. "Are you okay?" asked La'Ron.

"I wasn't going to tell you about this because I thought it would end soon. I've been having problems with this new kid named Shay who just moved in the apartments across the street from my house. He keeps bullying me and trying to fight."

"Why are you putting up with it?" asked La'Ron.

"He's much bigger than I am, and my uncle would whop me if he found out that I was around here fighting. Plus, I'm not a fighter. I'm a lover," Milton said, laughing.

"Well, you need to love practicing how to fight while you're at it," La'Ron said, laughing even harder. "When we leave school today, Milton, I will walk you home. If you want, we can stop by his house so I can let him know to leave you alone," La'Ron said, truly caring for his friend.

"Yeah, La'Ron. I think we should do that. I'm not trying to spend my summer worried about a bully." They both started laughing again, which was interrupted by the school bell, signaling that they had five minutes to get to their class.

"I wish we still had Mrs. Canada's class together. I'll catch you after school, Milton."

"All right. We all we got, later!" Milton replied.

As the day went on, La'Ron kept looking at the clock. It seemed that the day couldn't go by fast enough. He found himself thinking back on how the year went. Grade school was made up of about six different pee-wee football teams, and his team had taken the trophy that year with La'Ron playing quarterback. Over the years La'Ron and Mrs. Canada stayed close, and she always supported his football career and even went so far to getting La'Ron a personal tutor every summer. As he continued to think about the year ending and the fact that this would be his first year without a football tutor due to Mrs. Canada's sudden death, he thought about asking his grandma. But he knew she probably wouldn't be able to afford it. He also thought about the long bike rides he would have to take in the summer to spend time with his girlfriend, Latierra, who stayed on the east side of town. Even though it was easier to see her at school he knew the long bike rides would also help him stay in good shape.

Apart from all the questions Milton was asking him, La'Ron was really looking forward to meeting his mom and asking her questions. La'Ron had heard stories from his uncle about his dad and even worse stories about how his mom left him in a hospital and later selling him to his grandmother. He also felt that she was the only person that he could talk to about the time that his uncle had attempted to sexually violate him. As La'Ron sat there and replayed that day in his head, he reflected on how his whole family had taught him not to be a snitch. There was always this thought that if he said anything to anyone, he would be punished for telling. Luckily, Betty had pulled up to the house which scared his uncle straight. He never tried it again, but the reality was the damage was already done. La'Ron was known as a mannish little boy and even got suspended from school once for dry humping. The sad part is no one ever sat down to talk to La'Ron and try to figure out where this behavior came from.

La'Ron's train of thought was interrupted by the anger he felt every time he reflected on that day. He start mumbling to himself reflecting on the situation with Milton and Shay. "If Shay says anything I don't like about Milton, I'm going to start swinging." Shay was about fifteen pounds heavier than La'Ron and stood about a foot taller, but La'Ron felt he had the upper hand because he was in better shape than Shay. La'Ron also had already had a few fights around the neighborhood. Outside of his auntie Shanta beating him up, La'Ron was undefeated.

The final bell rang out and the schoolteacher yelled, "The year is officially over. Have a great summer, and for y'all that don't pay attention in class, I will see you in summer school."

As La'Ron was walking down the hall he could see Milton from down the hall standing at his locker, looking nervous.

"What took you so long?"

"I know you seen Latierra with me. I had to drop her off at her locker so I could get my kiss goodbye."

"Are you ready to go handle this?" Milton asked eagerly.

La'Ron began to laugh. "Chill out, Milton. I already told myself if he say anything I don't like, we are going to box. No matter what, if I am winning or losing, I don't want you to jump in."

"Are you sure, La'Ron?"

"Yes, I'm sure. We have been through this before, Milton. I've been raised to believe in fair fights. Win or lose, stand tall; that's the way you earn your respect."

As they got closer to the apartment complex where Shay lived, Milton spotted him outside around a group of guys who were hooking up some car speakers. "There he goes!" Milton shouted.

"Yeah, I see that. Be cool. I got this. Hey, Shay, let me holla at you real quick."

"What's good?" Shay asked as he looked at Milton as if he had an idea of what this conversation was about to be about.

"Hey, Shay, Milton told me that you've been bullying him, mean mugging and bumping into him. We both know Milton is not a fighter and he don't want no problem with you, so what's the issue?"

"There ain't no issue. I just don't like him."

"Look, Shay, that's cool and all, man, but—" Shay interrupted.

"But what, punk? Who do you think you are coming to my block checking me about your lil girlfriend?"

La'Ron threw a right jab, and all you could see was Shay's body falling to the ground. La'Ron followed with a left uppercut that lifted Shay back to his feet. Shay quickly grabbed on to La'Ron's braided hair, dazed but still able to maintain a firm grip. "Let go of my hair!" La'Ron threw a right hook and Shay hit the ground. He was out for the count. As Shay's mom ran out of her house, La'Ron and Milton took off running and laughing.

"Man, I can't believe he pulled my hair like a girl, and he got the nerve to call you my girlfriend. Look at how much of my hair he pulled out! My grandma is going to know that I was fighting. She's going to be tripping about my hair."

"Man, La'Ron, you really mess that dude up."

"Milton, you're all I got. You are like a brother to me. If anybody mess with you, they got to answer to me; and that is a promise that I will always keep."

"The feelings are mutual. I can't fight," Milton said, smiling, "but I will always be a loyal friend to you. Thank you for what you did back there. I'm sure he's going to think twice before he bothers me again."

"I agree, Milton. Well, I'm about to go home. I'll call you in the morning."

"I'll be over in the a.m."

As La'Ron walked through the door, his grandma was standing there with a belt. "Where have you been, La'Ron?"

"I've been…I was…I walked Milton home instead of riding the bus on the last day."

"And what else?"

"I came straight home, Grandma, I promise."

"Shay's mom just called me and told me you beat her son up."

"Honestly, Grandma, I didn't go there to fight; he started it. He's been bullying Milton for days now and all I asked him was to stop and he got to calling me names. You told me I should always stand up to bullies."

"Yeah, but that wasn't your battle to fight. Milton needs to handle his own problem or go tell his uncle and not you."

"Grandma, that's my friend…that's been my best friends for years."

"I understand, baby, but you can't live your life standing up for Milton. Now what if you would have killed that boy? You would be in juvenile prison while Milton would still be running around with his tail up his ass. I'm not going to whoop you this time, but if it happens again, your butt is mine. It's going to be a butt-naked you and a leather belt–swinging me. You got that, streetfighter?"

"Yes, ma'am!"

"But you're on punishment for a week, so you know what that means. Your butt better not leave this yard. Your mom called today and said that she will be here in two weeks. I and Ms. Debbie are going to box. Are you going to teach me some of your moves, La'Ron?" Betty asked, laughing.

"Nah, Grandma. I don't want it to be a butt-naked me and a leather-swinging you," La'Ron said, smiling. "I'm about to go to sleep. I'll see you in the morning. Love you, Grandma."

"Love you too, baby!"

As the morning rose, La'Ron woke up to the sound of who he knew was Milton knocking at his window. "Milton, is that you out there?"

"Nah, it's Shay! Of course, it's me, come out!"

"Hold up, I'll be out there in a minute." As usual, La'Ron could smell the good cooking coming from the kitchen. He headed to the bathroom to wash his face and brush his teeth, and on his way out the house he bumped into his grandma. "Good morning, Grandma!"

"Good morning, my butt. You better not leave this yard and don't think you're going to be running in and out my house all day either."

"I'm not, Grandma!" La'Ron said while rushing outside to speak with Milton.

"Hey, Milton, what's up?"

"Nothing much, just came over like I said I would to check up on you. Did your grandma put that leather to your back last night? Shay's mom called my uncle, so I know she called your grandma."

"Yeah, she sure did. Nah, she let me slide because I told her your scary butt was being bullied, but she did say I can't leave the yard for a week."

"That's a messed-up way to start the summer. We'll be in the fifth grade next year, and all this punishment and whooping that's going on have to stop."

"Yeah, with my grandma, it seems like grabbing that leather never gets old."

"Hey, La'Ron. What is your grandma cooking in there? It smells pretty good."

"Probably that discount swine from El-Roy's farm," La'Ron said, laughing. "Well, my mom will be here sooner than I thought. I'll be seeing her in less than two weeks."

"Yeah, that's cool, man. I'm happy for you. I can't wait to see my mom and dad either."

"Don't worry, Milton, When I get rich, I'm going to make sure you visit Nebraska."

"Yeah, if I don't get rich first!" Milton said, smirking. "Well, I'm about to go home. I just wanted to come check on you and thank you for yesterday."

"No problem, Milton, I'll see you tomorrow."

Two weeks later

"Today is the big day. How are you feeling, La'Ron?"

"I'm not sure, Grandma. I'm just ready to meet everyone. I see you've done a lot of cooking."

"Yeah, I'm going to give Debbie and the girls a taste of what they've been missing and show them Midwestern sisters of yours what real food tastes like."

La'Ron was looking out the window as the car pulled up with Kansas license plates. La'Ron ran outside, anxious to hug the woman who was his real mom. She was standing about five two, with chocolate-colored skin, nice long black hair, and a beautiful smile. She wore a lot of gold jewelry and had a fashion style that was unfamiliar to La'Ron's sight.

"Hi, son!" Debbie said as she ran toward La'Ron, picking him up and squeezing him tight in her arms.

"Hello, Mom!" La'Ron instantly started crying as he embraced the feeling of being in his mother's arms. "It's good to finally see you, Mom."

"It's good to finally meet you. I feel like we have so much to talk about. These two young ladies I have with me are your sisters," Debbie said, pointing at the two girls dressed alike, standing side-by-side, looking nervous as ever. "This is Pra'Shae," Debbie said, pointing at the tallest of the two. "And this is La'Che." If it wasn't for Pra'Shae being lighter in skin complexion, it would have been hard to tell the difference between the two. They wore matching outfits, had hairstyles with twists, and wore colored barrettes that matched their outfits. They also wore gold jewelry. They each had matching necklace with their initials and a gold ring. "La'Ron!" Debbie said, breaking his concentration on checking out his sister's style. "I'm going to spend some time talking with your grandma. Take some time to get to know the girls," Debbie said before making her exit.

Debbie watched from a distance on how well La'Ron connected with his sisters. In her mind, she couldn't shake the feeling of guilt for all those years that she had left La'Ron behind. Even though her intentions for making the trip back to Arkansas was to take La'Ron back to the Midwest with her, she knew it would have to be his decision to leave Arkansas and the people he had known to be his family behind.

"So, Mom," Debbie said, "tell me about La'Ron."

"La'Ron is a very observant young man. There's not that much to tell as he's still a child and all, but lately, we have been seeing a change in his behavior where he seems to get angry for no reason. I don't know what he's dealing with inside, but whatever it is, he hasn't talked to me about it. I've asked him on several occasions if he is okay or if there is something bothering him that we need to discuss, and he always gives me the same answer: 'I'm okay, Grandma!' I don't know. You know how these kids get when they start smelling themselves, and maybe that's it; he's just going through puberty. Overall, his grades are always good; he loves football and has won a few trophies. He runs around with this kid named Milton a lot. He just got in a fight a little while back over some kid bullying Milton, and he beat the kid up. The mom of the boy he was fighting called me crying. I wanted to tell her so bad that I hope her son learned his lesson," Betty said with a smile on her face. "I must admit I like Milton. I know they are good company for each other. Also, Milton lives with his uncle Anthony, who is raising Milton, and he's a good Christian man. La'Ron is very, very respectful. He's really a good kid. And wait till you see him play football; that boy can run to hell and back without being touched."

"Um," Debbie said proudly, taking it all in, "Mom, I'm about to go speak with La'Ron one-on-one. I'm going to send the girls in to help you set up the table."

"All right, sounds like a plan to me."

"Pra'Shae, La'Che, go help your grandma in the kitchen while I talk to your brother."

"Okay, Mom," they replied in unison.

Without Debbie even asking, La'Ron he went and sat down next to his mother as if he had been waiting on her to come back outside.

"La'Ron, how has everything been going?"

"Everything is good, Mom. I like my school, I like my friends, and I love being with my grandma."

"That's great! Do you have anything that you would like to ask me?"

"What was my dad like, and why did you leave me when I was baby?"

"I ask you to understand, La'Ron, I was a teenager when I got pregnant with you. I wasn't sure how to be a mom. Living here in this town got to be too uncomfortable for me. I felt judged everywhere

I went, and at thirteen, that was way too much for me. And if I'm being honest, the thought of being a new parent was way too much for me. I felt the only way I would ever get rid of the emotional weight that I was carrying was to leave this town behind, including you. Was that selfish of me? Of course! I didn't know what to do with my life at that time, but what I did know was that my mom would do a better job raising you than I could have ever done."

"What about my feelings, Mom?" he asked as the tears rolled down his face and off his chin. "Every time someone speaks about their mom, I feel uncomfortable, hoping that they wouldn't ask me about mine. Every time I get into an argument with one of the family members, they would always make statements like 'Go live with your mom' or 'Don't nobody love you, not even your mom, that's why she left you.' In those moments, I felt so much anger and hate toward you because, in my mind, I came to believe it was all true."

"I want you to know, La'Ron, that I truly love you and not a day went by that I didn't wonder how life must be for you mentally. Right now, you're too young to understand and maybe you never fully will, but the question we both should be asking ourselves is, how do we move forward? For starters, I would really like for you to move to Nebraska with me."

"My grandma Essie takes me to church every Sunday, and I have learned a lot about forgiveness there. What I will say is that I do forgive you, but I can't say that I will ever understand or won't have negative feelings toward you. I understand that you are my real mom, and I will always love you! And Nebraska? I thought you were living in Kansas?"

"Yes, I have been. Your sister's dad is from Nebraska, and he got some time to do in Nebraska prison. I've made several trips to visit him in prison, and we think it would be better for the girls if I moved there."

"So you can visit a man in prison, but it took you all these years to come see me?"

Those words made Debbie feel more shame than she had already been feeling. As the guilt appeared on her face, once again she thought back to the statement La'Ron made earlier about his church experience, and she knew that La'Ron was dealing with more childhood trauma than she could possibly imagine. "Well, La'Ron, we might as well put it all on the table. The truth is I don't know who your dad is; it's either Timothy Jackson or La'Ron Green. That's also a part of the shame I didn't want to face by staying in this town!"

"So I've been living with a lie my whole life. Where did the last name Jones come from?"

"I gave you that last name out of fear, out of doubt. Now that I look at you, I will say that you look more like Timothy. Your dad was a hardworking young man. He was very ambitious, smart, and family-oriented. Word was that he got involved with this petty hustler named One Shot. To make a long story short, he played a big role in your father's death. From what I heard, they say One Shot is still running around this town, so maybe one day you should build up the courage to ask him. I don't know much, but that's what I heard from the streets."

"You know, for all these years, I wondered what you were like. I wondered if you love me. Sometimes I even thought that my life would be better if I was with you. Oftentimes I blame myself for my father's death, because from the stories I heard, I understand that he was trying to make sure I had a decent life. I cried many nights just from the feeling of being alone. I felt like there was always a piece of me missing. I guess in all actuality, I've been depressed since I understood what a mother and father meant. It never helps seeing other kids with their parents, their parents showing up to their games, picking them up after school, etc. I've been searching for your love for years and I always seem to come up empty-handed, and now that you are here, I'm not sure how I feel. My grandma has been my mom all my life, and as of now I'm just not recognizing the difference I'm supposed to feel. I hope I'm making sense, Mom."

As Debbie was about to respond, Betty yelled out that the food was ready and for them to come in to eat.

"Okay, Mother," Debbie replied. "La'Ron, I understand that you are hurting and have been for some years. I wish I had a magic wand so I could change it all, but that's not how life works, son. From here on out, you need to understand that God is the architect of all human beings, and when he designed us, he understood the pressure we could and couldn't handle. Let this moment in your life help you understand how important it is to be a parent, a father. So remember this journey, your journey, when it's time for you to step up to the plate and be a dad."

"Yes, ma'am. I understand, Mom, but that leads me to one more question: Who is going to teach me how to be a dad since I never had one?"

"Okay! Let's go eat. We will talk more later, and I think you have a lot more growing to do before you have to worry about being a dad. But before we go, is there anything else that's bothering you personally?"

As La'Ron sat there thinking if he should tell his mom about what his uncle had done to him, he couldn't build up the courage to let the words come out. He replayed his uncle's words in his head. *I love you, nephew. You better not tell anyone.* Overall La'Ron feared what his uncle would do if he told, and he feared that his mom would force him to move if she found out.

"No, that is all for now."

As they all sat and ate dinner, the love was flowing in the room. Everyone was laughing and having the best time of their lives. It was one of those days when night came too soon, and it was a hell of a night for 12:00 a.m.

Betty watched as La'Ron was having the best time ever, still continuing to make connections with his sisters.

Betty noticed that the time was rolling by fast. "It's too late for y'all kids to be up. It's time for bed so us grownups can turn this party up," Betty said, already feeling tipsy off the few drinks she had at this point.

"Sit down, Mama, before you break something. You know, you don't got it no more. You can't move that thang like you used to!" Debbie said, feeling tipsy herself.

"Yeah, right!" Betty replied as she bounced down low as if she was picking up a gold bar off the ground before anyone else could get to it, but her reaction time of getting back up wasn't the same as it used to be. "Where is the carjack so we can lift all this butt up off the floor?" Debbie said. The house echoed with laughter from the dance move that landed Betty on the floor.

As La'Ron lay in the room with his aunt Shanta, his two sisters, and Jada a neighborhood friend, the sound of the downhome blues music and grown folks having a good time crept through the crack of the door.

"Are y'all asleep?" Shanta asked.

"No," they all replied in order.

"Do y'all want to play house?"

Pra'Shae and La'Che both replied at the same time, "What's house?"

Shanta explained, "I will be the grandma, La'Ron will be the dad, Jada will be the mom, and Pra'Shae and La'Che will be the daughters. First, we have to build a tent house with covers."

They all worked together, creating what turned out to be a big roof with covers tied to bunkbeds, tucked under mattresses and closed shut in dresser drawers. As the game continued, all the girls acted like they were cooking, waiting on La'Ron to come home from work. As he entered the tent with a bag as if it was a briefcase, he spoke to everyone inside.

"Hello, ladies!"

They all spoke back one by one.

"Hello, son."

"Hello, husband."

"Hello, Dad."

"Give me a kiss," La'Ron told Jada.

"A kiss?" she said with a confused look on her face.

"It's all a part of the game," La'Ron said.

Jada stood up and gave him a kiss as he requested.

"Ew, I'm telling Mama," Pra'Shae said, darting out of the room before anyone could stop her. "Mama! Jada and La'Ron are kissing!"

"Kissing!" Debbie ran into the room as if a pride of lions was chasing behind her. Betty followed. "What the hell are you doing to Jada, La'Ron?"

"I didn't do nothing! We were playing house."

"House? My daughters don't know nothing about them country bumpkin back wood games. Don't you know better than to be doing that?"

"We were just playing," said La'Ron.

"Just playing, my butt. Go to your grandma's room and take them clothes off so I put that leather on your back."

As La'Ron entered into his grandma's room, he thought to himself. that this will be the best time to tell his mom about what his uncle had done to him. "But maybe not," he mumbled to himself. "It might only make things worse."

As La'Ron entered into his grandma's room, it felt colder than ever. He had been in this room many times getting whooping, but not from his mom. He looked at the window to check if it was cracked open, but to no surprise, it wasn't because his grandma was crazy about not allowing bugs into the house. As he sat there staring at the door, he waited on the moment for his mom to burst through the door with his grandma's old-fashioned leather belt in her hand. "Jump out the window and run away!" he thought out loud. His thought was interrupted by two familiar voices coming from under the crack of the bottom of the door.

"Debbie, you know that boy didn't mean to do harm." It was his mom and grandma talking.

"Yeah, I know, but we need to teach him now that this type of actions are not okay."

"Well, gosh, why don't you try talking to him instead of whopping the boy the first day you meet him? How do you think he will view you after this?"

"I'm more concerned on how my daughters will view their brother. Something like this could scar my girls for a lifetime. Trust me, I know!"

As the debate continued between the two, La'Ron made his move, and out the window he went. He made his way through the backdoor steps and placed what he had been hiding into his shoe. He took one last look at the house before he ran as fast as he could without taking another look back. As La'Ron searched for his next direction he thought to himself this would be the perfect time to execute a plan he had been anticipating.

As his heart seemed to beat faster and faster with every step he took, it was this moment when the thought of being alone turned to fear, fear which he had never felt before. Not knowing where to run or who he could talk to, this was another moment that being a fatherless child only made the situation worse. As he thought about turning around, he could never forget how he always felt growing up in a home where he was loved but felt he didn't belong.

The more La'Ron ran, it seemed like the streets got darker and darker; and so did his heart. It was no turning back!

REVIEW BOOK CLUB QUESTIONS.

CHAPTER 4

Exposure

Knock, knock, knock.

"Who's there?"

"La'Ron, Betty Spencer's grandson"

As D-Low opened the door, he was confused looking at the young kid who was breathing as if he just ran a marathon.

"What's up, kid? What are you doing up at this time of night?"

"It's a long story. Can I speak with El-Roy?"

"Well, if you are asking to speak with El-Roy, you should consider telling me the short version."

"I ran away from home and I need some advice on what I should do about these feelings I am having."

"Well, I'm sorry to inform you that we don't invest in runaways, only throwaways."

"Well, I'm not here asking you to invest in me, nor am I here to sell you any guns. This is serious!"

"You are a smart kid. I wasn't expecting you to catch that line. You're Timothy's son, right?"

"As far as I know."

"You're funny, kid. Wait right here and I'll be right back."

D-Low was twenty-seven years younger than El-Roy, but he has been around the block for a while now, long enough to know that whatever this kid had on his mind was serious business. When D-Low was coming up in the streets he was a lot like Tim in many ways, but the major difference was he got money by all means. As D-Low's hustle progressed, El-Roy took a liking to D-Low and gave him a job collecting dues around the neighborhood. Around this time, he met the one and only person who was above El-Roy—Tony "3-piece-T" Jackson. Everyone around town called him 3-piece-T because since high school he wore color-coordinated three-piece suits. He was well respected in the community and was the type of man that believed in treating people with respect instead of making them fear him. But if you were to look on his face, his eyes may have told a different story. Some would say he had the eyes of a man with no soul. His pupils looked as if someone had drawn them in with a black marker. D-Low had seen this look in only two men's eyes: 3-Piece-T and La'Ron "Gat" Green; and now he was seeing this same trait when he looked into the young boy La'Ron's eyes. He knew this kid would be trouble in the future.

"Hey, El-Roy, 3-piece-T's grandson is out in the waiting area and he wishes to speak with you. He wouldn't tell me about what in particular, but he says it's very important and he only feels comfortable talking to you about it. And from the look on the kid's face, he means serious business."

El-Roy scratched his head. "Hmmm, that's Tim's son, right?"

"Yes! As far as he knows," D-Low said, imitating La'Ron.

"Bring him in and make sure you frisk him down good."

D-Low stepped out of the office confused. He knew El-Roy only frisks people down that are seen as threats or from the other side of the tracks. He didn't frisk guys around the neighborhood to show them a sign of trust. He knew there was something that El-Roy wasn't telling him, but he knew once the meeting was over El-Roy would inform him of what was going on. As D-Low walked out the room El-Roy sat behind his desk; he took his revolver off his hip and placed it on his lap.

"Come on, kid, El-Roy is ready for you. Turn around and put your hands up so I can search you for weapons."

"Weapons? I should be searching you for weapons," La'Ron said, smiling, excited that he was going to speak with El-Roy.

D-Low walked La'Ron to El-Roy's office wondering what could possibly be on this kid's mind. *Maybe he wants a job,* he thought to himself. *Nah, if that was the case, he would have went to one of the corner boys.* "Well, here we are, La'Ron."

"Hey, kid, so what brings you here in the wee hours of the night?"

"The word in my household is when people have problems, they come to see you. For the past few months my life has been hell—"

"Before we go any further, I want you to understand how conversing works in this room. One person talks and the other person listens. Don't rush, take all the time you need to express yourself, and be honest about whatever it is that's on your mind. After you're done, I'll give you the best advice I possibly can, and then we will see where we go from there. Understood?" El-Roy explained as he cut La'Ron words off.

"Yeah, understood, El-Roy!"

"Well, I'm sure you already know enough about my family history, so I don't want to travel too far down that road. Lately I've been feeling a lot of anger toward everyone in my family. I live in a house with eight other people, and I always feel like I'm overlooked, so I try to be everything that I see in my uncles that my grandma tend to be proud about. But I still feel like I'm not good enough. I love my grandma and always saw her as my mom, but deep down inside I know she's not my mom. I always had this thought of what it would be like to live with my mom and sisters, and along with that thought always came these feelings of feeling alone, feeling unloved, feeling abandoned. At times, the only thing that really takes my mind off this is sports and spending time with my girl and my best friend, Milton, but even then, I find myself still trapped in these negative thoughts. So today, or should I say yesterday, I met my mom and sisters for the first time, and for the most part everything went well. I asked my mom about my dad, and she told me that he was basically set up and this guy named One Shot was behind it all. In that moment I felt so much anger, anger that I have never felt before. As I shut my eyes to cry all I saw was red, which has never happened to me before when I was mad. In that moment I realized I couldn't feel hurt, only angrier. My mom wanted me to move to Nebraska with her, but I don't feel like I can leave and be at peace if I don't take One Shot's life away from him. Do you know him?"

"La'Ron, let me just say I can tell that you are a very wise young man, but before we continue, I have a serious question. What part of this story am I missing? What are you not telling me?" El-Roy said while looking La'Ron in his eyes.

"The other day my uncle groped me. I want to tell my mom what happened, but now they might think I'm making an excuse, so I don't get a whopping. I want to kill him too."

"Well...first, kid, let me start by saying that I know your grandma, and she is a damn good strong Black woman. I can somewhat understand why you might feel alone in a house where there are so many of y'all who need to be loved. Once again, you're a smart kid, so I'm sure you understand what it means to be responsible, which calls on us to be accountable and reliable. And I'm sure if you look at the bigger picture, your grandma is all three. I believe it's normal to feel how you feel, being that your mom didn't raise you growing up. Dealing with uncertainties and unanswered questions may cause you to feel alone, confused, and even angry. But understand just because someone hurt you, that doesn't mean our only answer to that problem is to hurt others. There's a saying that goes 'Hurt people hurt people.' That doesn't have to be your story, La'Ron. Long-term, I want you to understand how we choose to handle adversity says a lot about our foundation and character. Mentally you have to figure out a better way to manage that maze inside your head without letting anger or hurting others be the answer. One important thing I learned about taking a human life is there's always this ripple effect that's created, which means, not only does the victim suffer, his family suffers, the people who loved him suffer, the community suffers. Let's say you get caught now, not only do you suffer, but your family suffers as well. There is no winning in taking another human being's life. Understood?"

"Yeah, but a lot of people say you are a killer," La'Ron said, taking his eyes off the floor and into the center of El-Roy's eyes.

"Ha ha! A lot of people say a lot of things about me. Yes, a killer I am. In my mind I'm a justifiable killer," El-Roy said with a smile on his face. "I see killing as a way of discipline. Do that make it right? Of course not! When I took my first life, I felt similar to you, no love at home, I had so much anger inside of me that I couldn't control or had the advice on how to control it. I felt like as long as this man was alive there would be no happiness or balance in my life. The second man was behind your grandfather. Your grandfather was the best thing that ever happened to this town, the best thing that ever happened to me; he was my best friend and mentor. Anyway, I spent years waiting on the opportunity to hold his killer accountable. When your grandfather, 3-piece T, died I took over this town including the high-ranking police officer he had in his pocket. My chance came when the man who killed your grandfather got arrested, and for a large fee I worked out a deal with the officer to get me inside. I hung this man and made his death look like a suicide. I sat inside his cell with joy watching as he begged for his life, kicking, screaming, eyes rolling into the back of his head. His skin got darker, his body got stiffer, and I watched till he hung lifeless. Kid, I'm seventy-one years old, and now that I look back that was one of the hardest things I ever had to do. But for me, that was justice for 3-piece T. But what I want you to understand is that type of justice comes with a mental price tag that no one ever warned me about: sleepless nights, seeing demons, hearing demons, nightmares, and overall the ripple effect I spoke about earlier. La'Ron, have you ever saw a dead body?"

"No," La'Ron replied.

"Have you ever been to a funeral?"

"No, not one that I remember."

"Hmmm, have you ever seen two dogs fight till one dies?"

"I've seen stray dogs around the neighborhood fight, but I never saw any of them kill each other."

El-Roy yelled out for D-Low to step into his office. "Yes, El-Roy?"

"I want you to grab Casino and Nuke and prepare them to fight so I and the kid can watch."

"El-Roy, those two dogs are certified from the bloodline that One Shot left behind. We haven't fought those dogs in over a year. We only use them for breeding."

"D-Low, these dogs have made us plenty of money, right?"

"Of course!" D-Low replied.

"Okay, so in my eyes their job is done. We stand to lose nothing because everything that needed to be gained has been prolific and more."

"Yes, El-Roy, I understand that, but breeding dogs back into their dad or grandfather is the key to strengthen their bloodline. If we kill those dogs, that will set us back three, maybe four, litters, years!" D-Low closed his case with a smile and one last statement. "El-Roy, these dogs are like you; they have fought in plenty of rings and earned their respect to live a life of planting seeds."

El-Roy smiled back. "Even a respected killer deserves to be laid down for the right reason. Grab the dogs!"

"Okay, the dogs will be ready in thirty minutes, El-Roy."

D-Low was frustrated, but he knew that was an argument that he was not going to win. El-Roy wasn't in the dogfighting business, and he hated to watch them fight, so he understood El-Roy was trying to make a point at any expense.

El-Roy stood up and put his gun on his hip. "Look, kid, what you are about to see is never to be spoke on. Also, a lot has been said in this room that should never be repeated. Understand, due to the fact of who your grandfather was, I owe you all the guidance God will allow me to give you. There are multiple lessons that comes with what you are about to see, and what I want you to always think about is the importance of understanding the type of people you keep around you and the influence they have on your life, positive and negative. I also want you to understand that even a big portion of your life is all about choices. And even though our environment has the power to dictate some of the choices we make, always remember that some of the choices you make, you will have to live with for the rest of your life. Quick story: I spent a few years in prison in my early twenties, and I ran across some of the most amazing, influential individuals I have ever met. Most of these men had life sentences. I used to sit around and listen to their stories and also what led them to committing their crime, and trust me, it's the same stories of bad choices being made while under the influence or out of anger. Maybe it will be helpful to actually sit down and have a conversation with One Shot before you act off information that you heard. They say negative interactions are one of the major sources of turmoil, but it doesn't have to be that way. We have to stop continually judging people to the point it causes us to hate. We all share weaknesses, but more importantly we all share great qualities.

As El-Roy stood up to walk out the room, so did La'Ron. "Don't follow my lead, kid. Lead the way!" El-Roy said, making room for La'Ron to pass him. As they made it out the door they were met by a dark-skinned lady El-Roy referred to as Hershey.

"Hershey, can you call Betty Spencer to let her know that her grandson is here? I'm going to make sure he's home first thing in the morning. If she asks any questions, tell her I think it's best if we just give the kid a little time to think."

As they stepped out of the building, La'Ron noticed a four-wheeler that was sitting outside running that wasn't there when he came in. "This is our ride. Hop on, kid," said El-Roy.

As they drove for what seemed like every bit of ten minutes, La'Ron was amazed at the size of the property. As the gate opened to what seemed to be a large farm business, they drove passed small buildings after buildings, shacks after shacks, animals after animals, and a lot of cars that resembled a junk yard. As they entered a wooded area there were two guys standing next to a locked gate. At the sight of El-Roy the gate was unchained and opened. Inside was a huge red barn that was in dire need of a paint job. There was a sign that read "Slaughterhouse." In that moment La'Ron's heart started to race; the sight of the building made him nervous, but it was no turning back now.

"Let's go, kid…kid, La'Ron…hey!"

"Yeah, yeah, El-Roy, I hear you."

"Let's go, now is not the time to freeze up," El-Roy said, smiling.

La'Ron followed him inside and outside of school. This was the biggest building he had ever been in. La'Ron had never been inside a slaughterhouse, but he was thinking to himself, *This is one clean slaughterhouse, but the smell tells a different story.* As they walked toward the back of the barn, La'Ron noticed that most of the rooms were boxed in by plexiglass so he could easily see inside. There were mainly cows and pigs being slaughtered and hung on hooks. There was also a small room where chickens were being plucked and gutted. La'Ron had never seen so much blood in his life.

They finally arrived at two sliding doors at the back of the building. As El-Roy opened the door, the cold air rushed out from what appeared to be a large fridge storing milk. To La'Ron's surprise, El-Roy grabbed one of the milks which pulled as a lever, and as the wall of milk started sliding to the side it revealed a narrow passage that led to the basement. D-Low was standing on the other side of the sliding doors waiting.

"D-Low, where is Nuke and Casino?" asked El-Roy.

"Foot is grabbing them now, El-Roy. They should be here any second."

"Okay," El-Roy said, smiling. "I'm just making sure you didn't pack them up and send them off. I know how much those dogs mean to you."

Seconds later the dogs arrived. "Why don't they have ears?" asked La'Ron.

"They clip the ears when they are pups. When you're fighting dogs the ears can become a major medical problem that you can avoid just by cutting them off, and it also make their head look bigger. It's something they do to all the male dogs around here. There's no way to tell which one will grow up to be a fighting champ."

"Why don't they cut their tails?"

"The tail is a major part of their balance, kid. You should never cut a fighting dog's tail."

"El-Roy!"

"Yes, La'Ron."

"Earlier when we spoke you said you see killing as a form of balance, so why didn't you bring me down here so I could just watch you cut these dogs' tail off?" El-Roy and D-Low couldn't help but to burst out laughing.

Exposure

"You have the right idea, kid, but you are thinking about it the wrong way. The balance you are talking about serves no purpose. What's the point of cutting off a killer's trigger finger when he still has other fingers he could use? What's the point of cutting off a killer's hand when he can still call a hit? The only effective decision to be made is kill the killer."

"Hey, El-Roy!" yelled Foot."

"What's up, Foot, how is business?"

"Like Grandma's pecan pie, good as it can be! Who's the kid?"

"This here is La'Ron, 3-piece-T's grandson. Are we all ready to go?"

"Yes, sir!"

"Well, line them up and give me and the kid a show to watch."

D-Low and Foot prepared the dogs on the opposite side of the ring. As both doors snapped shut, the dogs instantly started barking and growling at each other. El-Roy nodded to Foot and D-Low, and they both hit a switch releasing the dogs. Both dogs rushed out in full speed, as the dogs worked their way around the ring mostly on their hind legs aiming to get ahold of each other's neck to secure the victory, La'Ron was watching in awe, and he never took his eyes off the ring. As he was watching the fight, El-Roy was mostly watching La'Ron, checking out his body language and facial expressions. To his surprise, La'Ron didn't flinch, not one time. El-Roy knew without the proper guidance this kid would grow up to be trouble. The fight lasted a little over a minute with Nuke taking the victory. As Casino lay there bleeding out lifeless, D-Low yelled, "Release!" and Nuke released off Casino's neck and went back to his corner.

"What did you think about that kid?" asked El-Roy. "Watch this, La'Ron, this the part you never get to see after dogs are finished fighting."

El-Roy nodded his head and D-Low let Nuke go. Nuke slowly walked over to the lifeless Casino, sniffed Casino briefly, and lay down right next to his lifeless body.

"Why did Nuke do that El-Roy?" asked La'Ron.

"From the moment each dog entered the ring they knew the only choice they had was to kill or be killed. It wasn't something they wanted to do; it's what they had to do. The most interesting fact, kid, is these dogs are brothers. Over the years there have been plenty of times I would be out riding my four-wheeler or one of the horses, and I would see D-Low out on the land with Nuke and Casino running free with no problems. But once you put them back in the ring, the mindset changes. The moment you put a gun in your hand and aim it at your target, you have no choice but to kill because if not, it's a great possibility that it will come back to haunt you. But the question I have for you is, why even put yourself in that mental space? You came to me not only talking about taking one man's life but two, and it's not because you had to in self-defense, for the safety or your own life. You just want to because you are hurting and you don't know how to deal with your emotions. Instead of trying to honor your dad by revenging his death, why don't you do something with your life to make him proud? Finish school, go to college, start a business, start a nonprofit in his name, and honor your dad in a positive way instead of causing somebody else's family to feel exactly what you are feeling right now—angry, mad, and hurt. Kid, I've given you all the advice I can in one day. Now my question to you is, will you be able to forgive your uncle and your father's killer?"

"El-Roy, if it's okay with you, I really don't want to talk about this anymore. I am starting to feel myself get angry again. But to answer your question, my only solution is to find a balance that will allow me to be at peace."

"Okay, kid, let's go. Hershey called your grandma and she knows that you are here, so do you want to stay the night or go back home?"

"I'll stay here tonight, El-Roy. I will leave first thing in the morning so I can take this trip to Nebraska with my mom. After talking with you, I think it's time for a new environment."

As El-Roy lay in bed preparing for his usual deep night sleep, he thought about the kid. It pleased him to know that he had helped La'Ron make his mind up on living with his mom in Nebraska. As El-Roy shut off the light, he said to himself, "That's one less problem I have to deal with!"

La'Ron lay in bed for hours replaying in his mind the conversation he had with El-Roy, but what El-Roy didn't know was La'Ron was preparing for his next move. As the loud snore crept under La'Ron's room door he knew it was time. He pulled out a 22cal. 2-shot Dillinger he had hidden in his shoe and headed for El-Roy's room.

La'Ron knew his mom was on the way to town and had decided that he would go back with her, but before he could go, he had to execute his plan. La'Ron manipulated his uncle into getting him a gun by telling him that if he didn't find him one, he would tell his mom what he had done. His uncle agreed to get the gun in order to keep La'Ron quiet. Growing up La'Ron had always heard stories about how a guy named One Shot was partly responsible for his dad's death. He knew that it wouldn't be hard to find One Shot because he was a heroin addict living on the streets, and La'Ron would even see him occasionally. When he finally found One Shot with the plan to kill him, One Shot gave him some more information as he pleaded for his life: that El-Roy was the one who ordered the hit on his grandfather, 3-piece-T, so El-Roy could take over the town. El-Roy even hung the hitman he hired. One Shot and D-Low had become best friends through breeding and fighting dogs, and one night D-Low confided in One Shot about how he feared El-Roy, mainly because he was the lookout guy the night the hanging took place at the police station. He couldn't understand how El-Roy allowed greed to take two people lives, even worse, one who had always been there for El-Roy and saw him as a brother. D-Low feared that he could be next and wanted One Shot to know in case anything was to happen to him. La'Ron knew One Shot wasn't lying, but he proceeded with his plan, releasing two bullets with a single shot from the double barrel Dillinger. It was time to find El-Roy.

La'Ron figured once he had the chance to get close to El-Roy he would tell him all about his grandfather, and he did. Surprisingly El-Roy revealed pieces of the story that One Shot had already told La'Ron. As he walked into El-Roy's room with his gun pointing in El-Roy's direction, he got close and pressed the cold steel to his head, waking El-Roy up.

"Woah, what are you doing, kid?" El-Roy asked.

"I know it was you who killed my grandfather in order to run this this city. Now you must pay," La'Ron said.

"Put the gun down, kid, and let me explain," El-Roy said, showing no fear but surely frightened inside.

"There's no need. I heard all I needed to hear—"

"Haha!" El-Roy laughed, cutting La'Ron's words short. "I should have followed my gut and killed you when I noticed you didn't flinch when those dogs were fighting. I guess I took you to the right spot; you and your family of killers are no different than those inbreed dogs. I see the permanent black look in your eyes, kid, that I saw in 3-piece-T's eyes. I know what time it is. You just better make sure you don't miss. Is there anything you want me to tell your grandfather and dad when I get to hell?" El-Roy said with an evil grin on his face.

"El-Roy, you once told me that even a respected killer deserves to be killed for the right reason. As I listened to you talk about the dog ring being an environment, I thought about my granddad. I guess when two people are associated with living illegal lives, regardless of how close you are your environment will eventually become toxic. Whether it's behind a female, disagreements, money, hate, or even greed, sometimes those feelings create irresponsible choices. You got to be careful giving out hypocritical advice because as you see it could be the same advice that get you killed. Oh yeah, tell my grandfather and dad that I love them, and I'll work on learning how to forgive. Oh, El-Roy, one more thing: thank you for helping me find my balance." *Boom*. El-Roy lay there lifeless as La'Ron disappeared into the darkness.

* * * * *

Once again, part 1 of this book is based on recollections of my childhood experiences. In the later chapters, you will continue to see the development and outcome of Milton's and my friendship. The unfortunate situation with my uncle was true as well. Might I add, me writing this book was not a bid for a popularity contest. If that was the case, I would have wrote about how

I was a ten-year-old having sex with my babysitter, who was well into high school. Sadly and surely, the stories of young men being involved with older women are given praise, high fives, and bragging rights and are even culturally accepted from a manhood perspective. Ultimately, long before I was able to identify it, trauma and turmoil were constantly being created when it came to those who were supposed to love me unconditionally, my family—my father, mother, and even my uncle. For a young mind, the context of love in your past can be confusing in your future, and that's why you see most young men who grew up in abusive households grow up hitting women. To my readers, I hope that you are truly able to appreciate my brave authenticity and how significant and impactful it is for me to share these stories. What if it was you? I think about the many kids suffering in silence regardless of what the situation might be, and for me, this is another one of my strategic approaches to encourage those on the power and healing behind speaking up and speaking out.

The moral of this ending is simple: be careful giving out hypocritical advice. Being able to forgive should be the only answer we have when it comes to revenging our loved ones' death, because one life lost can lead to so many others being hurt. Even though this story is very rough around the edges, it's very necessary to reach my target audience. For some of us it's unfortunate that we had to learn the hard way, and this story was just one version of what the hard way could look like.

I can't recall who thought it was a good idea to tell me details about my dad's death at such a young age, but one of my earliest childhood memories stems from around age five; and that was me knowing that my dad killed himself. I recall being a kid and the first time I thought about murder was not because someone did something to me, but because I knew my dad had murdered himself. Even though I never had plans to hurt anyone, but every time I thought about my dad—wishing I could talk to him, wishing he could pick me up from school, wishing he could watch me play football—those thoughts were always interrupted by his death because there were no happy moments created. So essentially, one way or another, from age five on up, I had murder on my mind. How real and raw is that?

    We can't continue to talk about *uncomfortable conversations* if we are scared to narrate the story.

REVIEW BOOK CLUB QUESTIONS.

PART 2

Autobiography

CHAPTER 5

The Transition

Minus the adversity growing up I became one of the popular kids, mainly due to me being good at football and being known as a pretty good fighter around the neighborhood. Football was a sport that I always enjoyed. We were allowed to play tackle football as early as second grade, which I'm sure might contribute to some of my brain damage. I played all the way up till eighth grade, winning two first-place trophies. For three years I played running back, and for the remainder of my sport years I switched to quarterback. As a kid I can recall being a football player as a major part of my identity. It was my sense of independence. I felt valued. I felt as if being on the field was where I belonged. I had dreams of someday being in the NFL. Even during the summers, my life consisted of playing football. I also enjoyed riding and fixing bikes, riding go-carts, four-wheelers, horses. And like most young men, I enjoyed flirting with girls around the neighborhood.

    I'm sure reading up to this point some would say I had it easy growing up, and honestly I would have to agree from the position that my grandma did everything in her power to make sure she raised me right. But if you know anything about being raised in a small Southern town, it's usually not the type of environment that allows you to fail. Everyone knows everyone, so even getting away with committing a crime was very rare. All my years of living in Dumas I can recall one murder that was committed. It happened right in

The Transition

front of my grandma's house, and my uncle even held the kid John-John who died in his arms from the A.K. bullet ripping through his body. And of course the perpetrator was caught. Aside of a few house robberies once or twice a year, hearing about people who broke the law was rare. These days I always hear the words *environmental circumstances* being thrown around, and I can honestly say coming from a small town to a bigger city like Omaha, Nebraska, there was most definitely some environmental circumstances that were new. And I personally believe one of the components that made my transition a challenge as well was this would be around the same time I was stepping into the age of being a teenager.

Also, there were gangs in Dumas, but I can't recall a single time a person was shot or, even worse, killed due to what gang they represented. Out of the five uncles I have on my mom's side of the family, four of them are Gangster Disciples, and they referred to each other as G's or Hoovers. My other uncle represented Play Boy Crip. In one way or another I found myself always trying to imitate them, so as early as third grade I told myself and them that I would represent both gangs and proclaim myself to be a Hoover Crip. But I guess this was another way of me searching for my identity and acceptance.

I really did enjoy every bit of my life growing up in Dumas; there's always this thought how I wish I would've never moved away. But the fact remains that there was always this emptiness inside of me due to the fact that I grew up without biological parents. As a kid, meeting my mom and two younger sisters for the first time is a moment that I will never forget. I'm sure in most cases you can equate my feelings to how you think you would feel if you met your favorite celebrity. Instantly I took pride in being a big brother, and in that moment I no longer felt like a motherless child. But days later she would pack up and go back to Nebraska, and I was left there once again feeling worse than I had already felt. Years later I got the chance to move with her, and I didn't hesitate to leave Dumas behind.

Now there was only one thing left to do, and that was to prepare for my transition mentally. Even as a kid I understood that I was leaving a lot behind, but at the same time I felt as if I couldn't continue to live life without my mom. As I; my mom, Debbie; my two sisters,

Pra'Shae and La'Che; and my mom's boyfriend, Larry, ventured on this journey to Omaha, Nebraska, I can't recall taking a single nap. Thoughts ran through my mind on everything and everyone I was leaving behind. Mostly I was thinking about my grandma who I had been calling Mom since I could talk. I was also thinking about my best friend, Milton, as the saying goes, he was truly my friend since the sandbox.

As I replayed some of the memories Milton and I had, I thought about all the times I had his back whether he was wrong or right. How in grade school we acted as if we were Master-P and Mystical from the rap group No-Limit, and of course I was Mystical. I would say the most memorable moment was the day we got baptized together. The older we got, the more we realized we had a lot in common. The most coincidental thing we had in common was both of our moms were living in Omaha. Now tell me how is that for a coincidence? Before I left, Milton and I had a conversation about him moving to Nebraska one day, and I even told him once I got rich that I would send for him. As those thoughts faded away and the sight of beautiful land, bright lights, big buildings, long bridges, and so many different waters along the way, it became more apparent that I was in awe of what life had to exhibit outside of Dumas.

After what I remember to be a nine- to twelve-hour drive, we had finally arrived in Omaha, Nebraska. When we arrived at our new living location, we pulled up to a house that seemed to be a machine, especially due to the fact that I had never seen or been inside a house with the basement attached.

At this point everything that I was missing as a kid, all those nights of not feeling loved by my mom, slowly faded away. I was no longer emotionally struggling with living in a house of nine trying to be a reflection of my uncles or imitate the things I saw them do that my grandma seemed to always approve of. I was also given freedom that I had never experienced. My curfew went from being home before the streetlights came on Monday through Sunday, till being out till nine o'clock on school nights and no curfew at all on the weekends. Overall, life was not bad, and financially we were doing okay. Larry had a tree service job making $20 an hour and would

The Transition

give me between $50 to $100 a week for doing odd jobs around the house. My mom didn't have a job, but I'm sure she received some form of state assistance. We had one of the nicest cars on the block, a fully loaded Jeep Cherokee. I'm not sure of the year, but it was dark green with tan leather interior tinted windows, alarm system, original factory rims, and a sunroof. Years later, after many nights of taking the keys to his jeep and sneaking out, I wrecked it. I never admitted to Larry to wrecking his jeep. I had told my mom, and she created a story saying that someone must have hit it while it was parked and kept driving, so I went with that. One great thing I can say about my mom when it came to her relationships is, she always made sure that her kids came before the man.

I soon realized not only was there change happening within the house, there was also a major change taking place outside the house, changes in which I have never experienced. The first house we lived in was located on Forty-Third and Ohio Street on the Northside of Omaha, in an area that was the hood of the Fortieth Avenue Crips but was occupied by an off-branch gang called Four-Trayz. I didn't have any problems in the neighborhood, and I adapted pretty well. At this point of time, I still had a thick country accent with a Southern swag that was new to the neighborhood. On top of that, I always had money due to my allowance I earned, and this allowed me to provide and not just be a free loader. I was also able to attract females that didn't usually come to the neighborhood. I had great leadership skills I adopted from being a quarterback, so I was always leading the way on what we would be doing most days. I believe because of all these things, adapting to the people wasn't hard.

Within my first week in Omaha, I met two guys from up the block, Anthony and Jamie, and we became everyday friends. Anthony was light-skinned, slim, funny, extrovert, known as a mama's boy. It seemed like everywhere he went there was someone there that knew him. He could always attract a crowd. He claimed to be a Blood from Twenty-Fourth and Lothrop Gang, but everyone knew he wasn't an active gang member and was just one of those guys that was tied in due to his family. He was the only Blood living in the Crip neighborhood, and for the most part he did well in the neighborhood because you could always count on him to have some good marijuana and host a clean dice game. Over time Anthony and I remained cordial but grew distant due to our different lifestyles.

Jamie Lee Highwolf (RIP) went by his middle name, Lee. He was a native from the Oglala Sioux Tribe. He had smooth red skin, long black hair, introvert, didn't gangbang, and had strong family values. Lee was less fortunate than Anthony and me, but he was an all-around hustler. Respectfully, he was the person that inspired me to tap into my hustler mindset. I remember on several occasions in the winter we went out to shovel snow for money, traveling to the west side of town to panhandle, and we also got our first job together selling discount candy for a higher price in rich neighborhoods for this guy named Stretch. Lee was the guy who kept the liquor flowing, and if we didn't have swishers to roll up, he always had his signature chrome and black marijuana pipe handy. Till this day, by far, Lee was the most loyal friend I ever had; he was one solid dude. He kept in touch with me during my incarceration all the way up to his death.

I guess some would say that we were known as the pretty boys around the neighborhood. I'm sure the catch was that females could look at us and pick a flavor. You had light skin, Anthony; red skin, Lee; and dark skin, La'Ron. Overtime, the three of us spent a lot of time partying, chasing girls, smoking marijuana, drinking liquor, and our favorite thing to do collectively was going shopping. Being around these two was the first time I had tried liquor or smoked marijuana. I would have to say this was the only downside to our friendship.

On one of our many missions to meet females, we stopped at this female named Ei's house. Lee was dating her. While they were in the room getting their groove on, I decided to sneak around and search for a rottweiler puppy I had seen a few days ago. In the process of me searching I spotted the dog sleeping in an unlocked kennel. So I took the dog and locked it in the jeep and waited patiently for Lee to finish getting his groove on. I remember going to the kitchen and making a bowl of cereal. At this point in my life, I had never robbed anyone, but at the same time I grew up around dogs and had a passion for them. On top of that, I had never own a rottweiler, and

The Transition

I always wanted one. There was just one problem I thought about as I made it to the bottom of my cereal bowl. I had to figure out a way to take this dog without her knowing 100 percent that it was me. I decided to leave the back door cracked and made it seem as if the dog got out the open door after we decided to leave. The plan was in motion, and in less than five minutes after us leaving, Lee's phone rang, and it was Ei crying asking about the dog. Obviously, Lee knew I had the dog and even expressed to me how he felt bad for Ei, but he assured her that we didn't take the dog and it must have slid out the door after we left.

After about three days of keeping the dog sheltered in the house, I decided to take it for a walk. While walking I ran across this older guy who I had known to be a Fortieth Avenue Crip. He called me over to a house where he was standing in the driveway next to a nice candy-blue Chevy on rims and asked me if I wanted to sell the dog.

"Nah, I don't want to sell the dog. I just got it myself," I said.

"I will give you $200 for the dog," he replied.

"Nah, I'm not trying to sell it."

"I will give you some crack cocaine for the dog, and I will allow you to sell it on this block when I'm super-busy, but under no condition you are allowed to exchange numbers with my customers. Even if you tried, I would find out."

I accepted. At this point it wasn't about the money; it was truly about me learning something new. And of course, the guy who gave me the crack, I saw him ride up and down the street several times with the nicest car and biggest rims in the neighborhood. There was this thought I had of me someday riding around in a candy-painted car myself, but I figured watching him that I had to hustle hard to get there. Also, I had heard about crackheads and had seen many of them around the neighborhood, so I knew it wouldn't be hard to get some money. I just needed to learn the dope game.

He showed me how to sell crack, how to use a scale, and advised me to bag it all up in ten-dollar rocks. He said after I sold it all that I could come back and buy some more and that he would sell me an 8 ball (3.5 grams=$350) for $125. And that's the story on how I got introduced into the crack game. But my simple mind took it a little further. I have a younger cousin named Q who looked up to me, and at the age of fourteen I convinced Q to sell crack for me. I told him that I would pay him $10 for every $100 he made me. Q was twelve years old when I first put him in position.

There was a lot I had learned in one summer, more good than bad. There were many new experiences I was exposed to that I couldn't imagine seeing in small town Dumas. And there would soon be another major factor that was about to be added to these combinations of new environmental life experiences, school, and gangs.

In Dumas there were only four schools you could attend in the whole town: Dumas preschool, grade school, junior high school, and high school. Go, bobcats!

The first part of these new environmental life experience was school. When I first entered school here in Omaha, North High School, I was amazed at how big the school was, and at that point in my life it was the biggest building I had ever stepped into. If I remember correctly, the school had three floors, including a basement and elevator. I must admit the size alone was a distraction. As time went on I adjusted to school pretty well, and a big part of that was due to the fact that Anthony, Jamie, and I all went to North High our freshman year. Ninth grade was easy as far as my attendance and grades went (shout out to Darianna H for helping me with my homework). When it came to school, football had always been a motivating factor for me, but looking at the atmosphere of North High I knew all that was about to change for me. Ninth grade was the year I gave up football, and I didn't even attempt to try out for the school football team, the Vikings. It's not an excuse, but I no longer had my uncles to look up to or my grandma cheering me on to play. On top of that, I'm now in a school setting where there were so many different varieties of females than I had ever seen in my whole lifetime. Like most young men stepping into their freshman year of school, females became my biggest distraction.

Before my freshman year I had already been dating a young lady named Keke. She was something new to my eyes. She wasn't an active gang member but had a gangster girl swag that I wasn't familiar with but found myself being attracted to. She had pretty dark skin,

The Transition

stood about five feet tall, had a nice frame, wore a lot of gold jewelry, kept her hair braided and styled in ways that I had never seen. Respectfully, she wasn't the only person that caught my attention on the block, but there were two things that separated her from the rest: her loyalty was second to none, and she was still a virgin. I also loved the fact that she respected her body. She made me wait years before she allowed me to enter her soul. For years, she was the love of my life, but as school continued, I grew distant from Keke, and all the late-night calls would soon come to an end.

While at North High there was another female catching my attention, Kyra. When I was a freshman, she was a junior. From the outside looking in, I could tell that she was popular around school. Her skin tone resembled what some would call yellow bone. She had fit frame and stood about five two. Her style was simple but always well-coordinated with a nice pair of Nike or Jordan shoes. She was known as a fighter due to her being a pretty good amateur boxer. At the time I didn't know any other juniors, but what I did know was that she stood out and I wanted her. In Dumas, due to me being good at football, I had a noticeable track record for dating popular girls, so now that I look back, I can see how dating Kyra was me converting back to what I would call good old habits. And being that I was a freshman and she was a junior, all my friends was surprised that she was my girlfriend, which in turn added to my popularity. Kyra became the first girlfriend I had at North High School.

And then there was Keyana Cotton. I believe one of the things that all people have in common is having a high school crush. Keyana was mine, and she is the reason why I believe in love at first sight. The first time I laid my eyes on her, I admired every inch of her body. She had pretty brown skin, stood about five four, and had pretty big lips; to sum it all up, in my eyes she was flawless. After doing my research I found out that she had a boyfriend, so I decided not to approach her. But I remember seeing her walk pass me and my friends one day in the hallway, and I told them all that one day she was going to be my girl. Of course they all laughed at me. To make a long story short, a year or so later I ran into Keyana at my neighborhood store, and we exchanged numbers. A few months later she became my son's mother. I guess I got the last laugh!

The second part of these new environmental life experiences was gangs. Once again, my freshman year at North High went well. I didn't make any enemies, but I did gain a few new friends. Along with that came invitations to house parties. The settings of an Omaha house party were new to me as well. A house party in Dumas was more like a family gathering and maybe a few neighborhood kids. Oftentimes the grill would be smoking, blues music playing through somebody's car speakers, old heads playing cards and/or dominos, loud talking, etc. But an Omaha house party was more like a freak show in somebody's mama's basement, and usually that same mama would be at the door collecting entrance fees. There was always a gun in sight, mostly female fights, but the best part was always the freaky dancing that was known as *break you off*. The overall goal when doing this dance was to be quick on reacting to each other's moves and continue this process until the end of the song. But if someone didn't make it to the end of the song, he/she ended up on the floor, stuck in a chair, while the crowd screamed and laughed. The person who broke off looked shameless. It was moments like those that made a good party great.

Growing up in the South I would always watch the elders two step or, as they would call it, "cut a rug." My grandma would often grab my hand and make me cut a rug with her, so I had a little rhythm which helped me when it came to mastering these new dance moves. Anthony was also a good dancer, and in no time, Lee became an okay dancer as well. Another perk to our trio was that we all kept money, so we would always show up to parties with liquor and marijuana, and ready to break any female off who thought she was the best dancer in the party, or at least accept the challenge. Even better, school was about to be out and that meant more partying.

During the beginning of the summer, I decided to start my own clique called *Da Crunk Boyz*. We were made up of guys who went to North High, who enjoyed partying and knew how to dance, and we even created our own style. We wore a lot of light pink in those days. Yeah, yeah, yeah, I know my readers are saying, "What? La'Ron wore

The Transition

pink?" Yes, I did. This was around the same time Cam'Ron from the rap group Dip-Set was wearing light pink and Da Crunk Boyz had it trending. We would go to the mall and get Crunk Boyz pressed on majority of our Tall-T's. If you didn't know us by our face, you knew who we were by our coordinated gear.

The Crunk Boyz grew faster than I imagined. Since we operated as a clique, there was no initiation process outside a person getting approval from Anthony, Jamie, or me. We were made up of all different hoods and gangs, Crips and Bloods included. Within the first summer we went from us three to more than thirty members, and this was just the beginning. The first summer went well—no fights, no shootings, just a whole lot of partying. To complete my summer, I felt like there was one trend I was missing out on that I had to add to this new character I was creating, and that was to put some gold in my mouth. I still had my small hustle going on which had spread outside of Miami park, so I took $300 to the Cross Road Mall and bought myself a four-piece 10kt grill. Now I was ready for the tenth grade.

The beginning of sophomore year was a lot different from my freshman year. A lot more people knew who I was, and I found myself gaining and accepting a lot of new friends. That same year a Crunk Girlz clique established themselves. There had already been a squad of females around Miami park claiming Crunk Girlz, but they didn't go to North High School. They operated the same as the Crunk Boyz clique: females made up of different hoods and gangs, Crips and Bloods. A female by the name of Cody from Twenty-Ninth Street led the way for the Crunk Girlz, and even though Anthony and I as leaders never established a leader, we felt okay about it all because Cody was representing hard. As the cliques kept growing, so were some of my personal friendships. I took a liking to one of the younger guys who joined the Crunk Boyz, Akeem Jones (convicted to life in prison), who went by the name Savage at the time but later changed it to Grimy. I can't recall exactly how we met, but I'm guessing it was through a class we had together. For me, one major factor that drew me close to him was because we both had the same last name. In addition to having mothers that struggled with addictions, we had sisters that we cherished, and he stayed by my hip, so in no time we were calling each other brothers.

Akeem is a few months younger than I am, had stockier built, dark skin, and stood about five six, with a gap between his two front teeth that he embraces from an African cultural perspective. Akeem was one of those kids that really had it hard growing up, and like most kids who are not affirmed in their household, he was in the streets searching for acceptance and his identity. I'm not sure what Akeem saw in me, but I know we were inseparable. If I had it, so did he; and vice versa. Aside from all the personal attachments, we also shared a street perspective. We both represented Crip. Earlier in this chapter I told you how I was introduced to gangs, so this is where it all came together. Once again, it was around third grade when I self-proclaimed myself to be a Hoova Crip. All the way up till about sixth grade, I didn't know Hoova Crips was actually a gang across the United States, nor did I know that it existed in Omaha.

So one day, I got home and my mom informed me that we would be moving to a new house at the end of the month, and guess where we moved to: in a neighborhood that was the territory of the Thirty-Seventh Street Hoova Crips. We moved into a house that was in the heart of their neighborhood on Thirty-Eighth and Meredith Street. A short time after was when I met Tenn, Doe-Boy, and Blue (RIP). They were the first Hoova Crips I met in Omaha.

Now that I look back, I would have to say environmentally this move was the second worse transition in my life. The life of the fun, carefree young Crunk Boyz was fading away, and a new character was being developed. Within weeks of moving into the new neighborhood, I traded in my light pink Crunk Boyz logo gear for royal blue Tall-T's and hoodies.

REVIEW BOOK CLUB QUESTIONS.

CHAPTER 6

The Birth of Clown

One day after school Akeem approached me and told me about an altercation he had going on with some Bloods at school. Due to the Crunk Boyz clique, Akeem knew I had a few friends that were Bloods, but he also knew I looked at him like a brother. I can't recall what the issue was about, but I do remember Akeem asking me clarifying questions.

"Are you on my side or theirs?" he asked.

"You don't have to ask me that question. You know I'm riding with you," I said.

So at the end of the school week, we all agreed to meet up after school for Akeem and Chris to fight. Chris was known as a Victor Street Blood. At the end of the week everything went as planned and the fight took place. Akeem whooped Chris so bad, it seemed as if the fight was in slow motion. With every punch came a loud thump followed by the crowd making all kinds of sound effects as each blow was landed. Chris didn't get a punch in.

When we got back to school that following Monday the tension was high, and the way Chris got whooped we knew it wasn't over. After a long debate of what would happen next, the next fight was set and now it would be my time to box. We all agreed to meet up at a spot that was located about ten blocks away from school. I didn't know which guy I was going to fight, but I do remember telling myself losing was not an option. Early on in the hood, I was known to be one of the best physical competitors; if you ask me, I was second best after Blue. We would often battle each other which included a lot of shadow boxing, body shots, and body slamming, but this would be my first real fight in Omaha. When we made it to our meeting spot to fight, the Bloods lined me up to fight this guy by the name of D. Our fight ended with me landing a three-piece combination which resulted in D being knocked to the ground, hitting his head on one of those iron circle sewage lid. D was transported to the hospital where he was in a coma for weeks and ended up having to have surgery on his jaw. In that moment I felt like I had honored my gang, put in some work, earned some stripes, improved my reputation, and drew the line that we were not going to be pushed over.

The next day when Akeem and I arrived at school, we were met by the school police officer with his firearm drawn telling us that we had been expelled and weren't allowed back on the school campus. I'm not sure the exact amount of time D was in a coma, but I do recall detectives coming to my house questioning me, telling me I better hope D didn't die. Thank God he didn't; once again, he managed to live and I didn't see another detective pertaining to the fight.

Even though Akeem and I were expelled from school, the fighting wasn't over. Our neighborhood was located literally across the street from North High School, so every day after school we would stand across the street mugging and throwing up gang signs at the Bloods that would walk by after school. It never escalated because there always seemed to be police officers in sight. I must admit even though the Bloods couldn't whoop us one-on-one, they weren't backing down. But one thing was clear: there was no one willing to fight us one-on-one.

After a few conversations we all agreed to meet at Fontanell Park for a gang fight. If I had to guess, I would say the fight was fifteen-on-fifteen, no guns, no knives, no weapons at all, just a field full of hard hitters. The fight lasted for three to five minutes, which seemed like forever, before the police finally arrived, and we all scattered like roaches. Afterward we all got together to celebrate what we saw as another victory. That night we drank a lot of M.D 20-20. We laughed for what seemed like hours about what took place, not only about that day, but some of our past experiences as well. Blue found himself at the forefront of these conversations, especially that he was the one who usually did the most damage. But that day, Blue knocked out at least three guys by himself, including the biggest guy on the Bloods' side who went by the name Lance. I always recall the fact that Blue would say that he blacks out when he fight. That was Blue the knockout champ of the group. Rest in peace, his soul!

Being out of school was another new experience for me as well. Since the move from Miami Park, my drug connection slowly faded away, so did my hustle, and even worse my friends Anthony and Lee. Akeem and I found ourselves running around the neighborhood getting in all kinds of trouble without getting caught. We were robbing stores to eat, breaking in abandoned houses, sneaking out the house late at night, and even picking up a few recruits along the way. Being out of school and spending more time in the neighborhood allowed us to be exposed to new elements of the gang life. I would say one of those elements was learning the history of the guys that came before us, the Thirty-Seventh Street legends. Stories of the top hustlers; killers; who had the most money, the nicest cars, the finest women; who died and why; the snitches; and my personal favorite stories of *real n*ggas*. Once again, we didn't have any OG's in Thirty-Seventh Street leading the way for us due to most of them being caught up in the Federal Inditements in the late 1990s and early 2000s, including the few who were locked up for murder. So early on all we had were these stories to look up to. To name a few, I admired stories of guys like Bumpy, T-Stubb, Nutts, Butts, and my personal favorite, Bernard "Nardo" Long (convicted to serve life in prison, published a book titled *Vision Now*). Overtime I would always compare myself to Bernard, a young fly guy leading the way; keeping the nicest cars; getting money, nice women, a lot of respect in the hood; quick to fight; quick to shoot—overall just a real street dude that mostly everyone respected and liked. But along with these stories another element of the streets was clear; and that is, if you wanted to survive in the streets, you better have a gun, and around this time we didn't have one.

In addition, all the fights—on top of guys that we would beat up for walking in our neighborhood—opened the door for me to feel fears that I had never experienced before. There were those stories about guys being shot or losing their life and also conversations about protecting the neighborhood. With that there's this saying, "You rather get caught with a firearm than without a firearm," which means I would rather have the police catch me with a firearm and I fight it in court or spend a few years in prison instead of having one of my enemies ride up on me and catch me without a firearm and kill me. There was a time when I would walk through my neighborhood carrying a backpack that held a paintball gun that didn't work but looked similar to a TEC-9 machine gun. After flashing it one too many times without firing it, I knew that this could become a problem if I ever found myself in a situation really needing to use it for protection, and once again there were no OGs to supply us with any.

Once again, I would find myself at the forefront of finding a solution to our problem. On a few occasions, my mom took me to her brother's, my uncle, house with her, and through these visits, I learned that he enjoyed hunting. Even better, I discovered he had a gun cabinet full of guns. There was an upward of ten guns, more than I had ever seen in my lifetime. After having a conversation with my uncle about my interest in going hunting with him, I figured out his work schedule, and that's when the plan went into effect in my head that I would break into his house. The day came for me to execute the plan.

It was a cold early morning around seven o'clock, and there I was standing at his back door with a duffle bag in hand, making several attempts to kick the door down before it finally swung open. I didn't waste time, and I knew exactly where to go and what I was looking for. As I was robbing my uncle, I must admit I felt guilt. I felt so bad I remember telling myself that I wasn't going to take all his guns. But at the same time I was thinking about my friends' life and mine and how we really needed these guns to protect ourselves. Back to the neighborhood I went running with a smile on my face but nervous as can be at the same time. I still remember the devilish look on the guys' faces as soon as I opened the duffle bag, revealing the guns inside. This was another moment I felt I had honored my gang, put in some work, earned some stripes, and improved my reputation. Any house party that we knew about, we made sure we showed up screaming "Hoovas!" as loud as we possibly could, and the looks on our face and the visible 12-gauge pump dared anyone to challenge what we stood for. Even though back then we were only shooting in the air, it was effective. The sound of a 12-gauge shotgun would make a giant stop in his track, so just imagine the fear of a teen, someone who would hear gunshots for the first time.

Some may ask where my mom was at when all this was happening. Out of respect for my mom, I'm not going to make an effort to tell her story outside of me and her relationship. But as time continued, I noticed that my mom and Larry spent more time in their room. I was seeing them less and less. The refrigerator started to be empty toward the middle of the month due to them spending less money on groceries. Bills were going unpaid and would sometimes get cut off for a couple days. I would often overhear Larry having conversations with his boss on the phone yelling about continuing to borrow money before payday. Also, my allowance had stopped. The truth was I was so deep in the streets. I missed the signs that something was obviously wrong at home, but like they say, what happens in the dark will come to the light.

One day after a long day of running the streets and patrolling the neighborhood, I went home for the night and noticed the rifle I kept in my room under my couch was missing. After taking a look around the house, I noticed that nothing else was missing, and I suspected my mom had found the gun while searching my room. I thought about going to ask her where my rifle was, but my mom is the type of person that address all issues, so I figured as soon as she knew I got home that she would be questioning me about why I had a gun in the first place. To my surprise, when I woke up the next morning, I still hadn't heard a word from my mom. I remember telling myself to get up and leave before she woke up, which I did. After another long day of patrolling the neighborhood, when I arrived home, I was greeted at the front door by my uncle that I had robbed. I knew what time it was, but I was also thinking to myself there was no way he knew it was me.

"My house got broken into. Have you heard anything about it?" he asked.

"Nah, Unc, I haven't heard nothing," I said.

"Your crackhead mama tried to sell me one of my guns, and she said she found it in your room!" he said, looking me dead in my eyes. "You don't have to lie. You don't have to admit it, but I'm going to tell you now stay away from my house, my family. And if I ever see you around there again, I promise the outcome is going to be very bad."

In that moment I had a lot running through my mind. I can't recall how many of my guys I had with me that night, but I do recall Blue being there, and he kept giving me this face searching for my approval to shoot my uncle, which I didn't give him the head nod to do so. I'm more than sure my uncle had a gun on him as well, but us killing each other was the last thing on my mind. The truth was I was tripping off the new information I learned about my mom being a crackhead, and as I'm reflecting back on the thoughts of my mom being on drugs, everything was starting to make sense. Once again, I was so deep in the streets that I missed the signs. I was standing there feeling like a motherless child all over again. I was also dealing with the feeling of being betrayed and knowing that I would never be able to trust my mom again. That same night I packed my duffle bag full of clothes and ran.

Truthfully, I was so hurt by my mom's actions. I felt like running away was the only way to make her feel my pain. It was a cold fall night when all this took place. There was an abandoned house in the neighborhood that had electricity with an electric stove inside I used to keep warm. So for about a week that's where I slept, in an abandoned house on a kitchen floor. I recall my mom blowing my phone up begging me to come back home and promising me that she wouldn't punish me and that things would change around the house. After so many cold nights of being hungry, robbing stores to eat, breaking in one of the guys' grandma's freezer that was in her garage, sleeping on the hard floor, I decided to go back home. On top of all that, I was also missing my annoying little sisters.

The Birth of Clown

My young mind was telling me that there was one more thing I needed to do before going back home, and that was to talk with this older guy named Slope (RIP) who was an OG from Fortieth Avenue Crips. Slope had a sister that lived in our neighborhood named Nina, and we would often see him there. Slope took a liking to us and would come around giving us hypocritical advice and selling us our marijuana. As we sat down and talk, I told him about the whole situation between me, my mom, and my uncle and how learning this new information of her being on drugs was affecting me. As he fired up the PCP stick, he explained to me the difference between a crackhead and a smoker.

"A smoker is someone that you wouldn't be able to tell that they were using drugs by looking at them. They worked, had houses, ate, and kept their weight up, didn't run the streets. Oftentimes they paid their bills on time, then on the weekends they might spend a few dollars with the dope man. These are people who somehow had control over their habit, well, at least managed it. A crackhead is the complete opposite, and you could tell by looking at them that they use drugs. They are usually street runners who did almost anything for their next hit of dope. I think you should go home and talk to your mom about how you're feeling. God only gives you one mother. Find a way to forgive her!"

When I got back home, my mom and I had a long conversation. The talk ended with her giving me this story about how she feared for my life and how she wanted me to go back to Dumas and live with my grandma. But she also assured me that I could come back when I was ready. I agreed, but overall I really didn't have much of a choice. It was either her way or run away again and find myself sleeping on a hard floor. And there was also the thought of how good it would be to see my grandparents and my childhood friend, Milton.

Of course the first day I got there my grandma had set some rules for me that I had surely outgrown. I would spend most of my time with Milton, telling him all about Omaha and my experience there. He told me that he was still in contact with his parents who lived in Omaha, and they were having talks about Milton being able to visit soon. I reminded Milton with a smile on my face, "Don't worry. I told you when I get rich that I'm going to send for you." One thing is for sure, being back in Dumas had become too slow-paced for me, and I had no aspiration for staying.

While I was in Dumas I kept in touched with the guys back in Omaha by phone. Often I was introduced to some new recruits who said they had heard so much about me and couldn't wait to meet me. I told them the feeling was mutual. A few months later when I got back to Omaha, I was surprised by how so much had changed in a short period of time. Not only did I meet some of the new recruits. I also met some of the older guys that started to come back around and even a few that had got out the Feds. To name a few, C'ion (RIP), Fatts (RIP), E-Bo (RIP), NoNo (RIP), Penny (RIP), Savo (RIP), Maxxo (RIP), Mook (convicted to life), Cin-Loc (convicted to de facto life sentence), Jean-Jaccet, Boston, LD, Floyd, Big-Foot, D-Boe, P-Locc, Light-Bright, Mario, Big Caine (RIP), Blue-Falcon, Nephew, Tycoon, KK, Jessica, Keke, Teara, and a guy who would become my new best friend, Jovan Reed, a.k.a. Nightmare (RIP). And there were many more that came along the way.

From the jump I noticed how the dynamics in the neighborhood had changed and how there was a pecking order. Words like BG (baby gangster), YG (young gangster), and OG (original gangster) were being thrown around. Before I went to Dumas we all moved as one. We didn't subscribe to labels such as G's because we saw each other as brothers. I also noticed the cause of this change was due to the old heads that were hanging around. I also noticed that there were more guns, crackheads, and trap houses in the neighborhood. In our earlier days I had always led the way, and I noticed someone else had filled my shoes, leading the way for the BG's. Nightmare! I thought it would have been Akeem, but it seemed that he was always stuck in the system, in a group home or Douglas County Youth Center (DCYC). From the jump Nightmare and I took a liking to each other, and I liked what he projected and how he stood up for the youngsters. Since he was a few months older than I was, I envisioned myself playing the same role.

Due to my past experience of selling drugs and Nightmare having a consistent connection on crack, it didn't take me long to work my way up. Like others, I would pick a spot in the neighborhood on Thirty-Fifth and Grand Street, and as cars pulled up we race to them one by one. Another thing that had changed when I got back to Omaha was that I had no curfew, so this afforded me the time to be in the neighborhood late nights. Oftentimes it would be Akeem, Blue, and me. I would be serving while they were looking out.

It was a nice sunny day outside, and as usual we were all in the neighborhood on Thirty-Fifth and Grand Street. I can't recall what the occasion was, but I do remember there being more people on the block than normal. It was a normal day: females running around, hand guns being gripped, rifles and shotguns being stashed, rap music playing through somebody's car speakers, liquor and marijuana being passed around, and multiple cars pulling up to get their fix. As we all raced to the cars, I got the jump on this white car that pulled up with a White man behind the wheel. My first thought was that he looked like a police officer, but that thought disappeared quickly as he flashed two crispy twenty-dollar bills. I broke him off then stashed my sack back in front of a house that was about five houses down from where we all gathered. As I was walking back toward the crowd, all I saw were police cars coming from all directions. In a matter of seconds, I was apprehended and damn near stripped naked in the middle of the street. To their surprise, they didn't find any drugs on me, so they had to let me go. But once again, there were so many police officers I didn't notice that they had found my sack and put it back in its proper place. After they let me go, I waited about a half an hour before I decided it was time to go back and get my sack. I recall one of the older guys, Lil Poccet (convicted to life), telling me that it was too soon and that I should wait, and of course I didn't listen. I took a few minutes to scan the block, and I didn't see a police car in sight, then I made my move. Soon as I picked up the sack I noticed that some of my crack had been taken out. I instantly dropped the sack, and as I turned around to walk away once again there were police cars coming from every directions. Once again they didn't find the sack on me, but they had been watching from a distance and saw me grab it and throw it back down.

June 30, 2006, at sixteen years old, I was arrested and charged with possession of crack cocaine. They took me to an interview room and questioned me about the purity of the crack and how did I get such good quality at a young age, and more importantly they wanted to know where I got it from. I recall giving them this story about getting the crack from three midgets on a skateboard, a bogus name and location, but they knew I was lying and took me straight to DCYC. Since it was the first time I had been in trouble with the law, I was released on a signature bond.

As I was waiting on my mom and Larry to pick me up, I was 100 percent afraid of what she was possibly going to do to me. I, for sure, thought she would create some new rules around the house, cut me off from seeing my friends, move neighborhoods, and even worse send me back to Arkansas. I also recall this being the first time I thought about stepping away from the gang life and changing my ways. As I walked to the car with my head down, I thought about running to avoid having the conversation with my mom.

"Are you okay?" my mom asked.

"Yes, I'm okay!" I replied with a dry tone.

"If I knew you were selling crack, I would have been buying it from you," she said.

Outside of the Sir Charles Jones playing softly through the speakers, the remainder of the ride was silent. As I sit here and write this, I can only imagine the conversation my mom and Larry had on the way to come get me. Here I was scared, thinking about changing my life, stopping selling drugs, staying away from the hood, and even better, focusing on my education. In that possible life-changing moment, I went from thinking about change to now thinking about the amount of money that I could possibly make, especially knowing that Larry was making $20 an hour working. Sad story, but 100 percent true. Often when you hear these kinds of stories of moms finding out their kids were hustling, they got kicked out of the house or their parents had their hand out constantly asking for money. As you see, for me it was different, and I was so confused! But for the record, things wasn't always bad with my mom. She kept a roof over our head, every Christmas we had gifts, every Thanksgiving there was a hot meal, when school started we had new clothes. She just had a demon on her back that she couldn't shake.

Soon after I got home I went straight to the neighborhood where I was welcomed back with open arms, liquor, marijuana, a new sack, even a few jokes being thrown my way about how stupid I was for going back to get the sack after I was warned not to, but even better, a little bit more respect on my name. Since my arrest, no one in the neighborhood had been arrested, so this was a sign that I didn't snitch. Personally, this was another moment I felt like I had honored my gang, earned some stripes, and improved my reputation.

But there was one thing that I couldn't get off my mind. I couldn't stop thinking about the amount of money I could possibly be making serving to my mom and Larry. Once again, I decided to seek advice from Slope, and I remember word-for-word the advice he gave me.

"If you don't sell them the dope, then someone else will. Why not keep the money in your household so you can help provide for your sisters and look out for yourself at the same time?"

And that's exactly what I did. I went from making $250 to $300 before re-up, to now making $625 to $675 a week before re-up. Essentially, profiting $1,000 a month. This also afforded me the opportunity to deal less with crackheads and build a clientele of stable smokers, which meant I was no longer hustling on the corner full-time and was now working off a phone that was guaranteed to ring at least once every thirty minutes with a client on the other line ready to spend $20 or better. Throughout my years of hustling I had clientele that were stay-at-home moms, two different car salesmen, high school coach, cable company man, two retired schoolteachers, veterans, a musician who played for a known local gospel band, a realtor, mechanics, and of course I kept a few street runners of women who prostituted in the streets. But my most profitable clients were a handful of nurses and bikers, mainly the bikers because they always threw parties with other bikers coming in from all different states ready to spend money and get high.

During this time in my life Nightmare and I became best friends. Even though I was doing well I still looked up to him. We had a lot in common and motivated each other in many ways. He wore silver jewelry; I wore gold. One summer we had matching smoke gray PT Cruiser cars, matching firearms. We wore our hair braided in the front with singles in the back with beads. We would often ride around in separate cars following each other. We even got our baby mamas pregnant at the same time with boys. For a long period of time our days looked like riding around making crack sells and meeting women.

    Everything was going well around this time, and I would also meet the second love of my life, Tatianna. She was the first female I dated where I felt like she was out of my league. Everything about her screamed five-star chick: pretty soft brown skin, slim frame, big breasts, had her own car, own money, own house, and she was even the first girl I dated that wore skirts and high heels. Even better, she knew I was seeing other females, but regardless of what I had going on in the streets she was always there for me. All the way up till my incarceration in 2014, I had a key to her houses and didn't even live there. She was my rider, and if I won the lottery I would trust her with the ticket.

    Around this same time, in the winter of 2016, Nightmare would meet a new female as well, but there seemed to be one problem: she had a boyfriend. We would soon find out that her boyfriend was from Thirty-Third Street Mafia Crips, and he was not happy about Nightmare taking his girlfriend. It's my personal opinion that the Thirty-Third Street Crips is in the top two most dangerous hoods in Omaha. From this moment on, our everyday lifestyle of chasing money and women would no longer be at the forefront of our day. The beef had begun!

REVIEW BOOK CLUB QUESTIONS.

CHAPTER 7

Post-Traumatic Street Disorder

The Thirty-Seventh Street Hoova Crips has always been one of the smallest hoods in Omaha. Now we had beef with the biggest hood in Omaha. Even though we had many gang members from Hoovas, not everyone was gangbanging. Back then we referred to each other as goons. The goons consist of me, Nightmare, Savo, Grimy, Blue, and a handful of others that would follow shortly after. Throughout our years, we would also gain new enemies. It always ended up being against hoods that were two times bigger than ours: hoods such as Twenty-Ninth Street Killer Park, Fortieth Avenue Crips, and our rivals since before my time, the Twenty-Ninth Street South Family Projects.

One thing we didn't realize was how much these conflicts was going to cost us. We would go on many high-speed chases throwing guns out the window, which in turn resulted in us having to buy new ones, on top of bullets, beams, and even a few traffic tickets if we got caught. But the same way we were hopping in cars looking for our enemies, they were doing the same. The uptick in shootings in our neighborhood caused us to lose some of our clientele. I guess when you look at it from the crackheads' perspective, they didn't want to be in the middle of a war zone; they just wanted to get high. The most expensive part of it all was buying and renting cars due to them being shot up or due to us switching them up to keep our enemies guessing.

Around this time I had a client who worked at a cable company. He introduced me to this White guy who worked at a car dealership, who was also a smoker. This seemed to be perfect timing to a solution that I was having a problem with. After getting to know the car dealership man better, he assured me that he could get me any car off the lot I wanted for half price, if I paid cash. But there was one catch: the car had to be in his name because that was the only way his boss would allow him to get the discount. If I'm being honest, from the jump I felt something was off with this guy from the dealership. But I had been dealing with the cable man for years, and I never had a problem with him. Even the few weeks I had been dealing with him, he always paid his debts on time. I agreed to the deal under one condition: he had to sign a paper with both of our signatures included, stating that he gave me permission to drive the car. He agreed, and I told him that I would meet him the following week with the money.

At this time I was seventeen and still living in my mom's basement. We were living in a nice-size house on the corner of Forty-Fifth and Bedford Street. The basement had two rooms: one room where I slept and another room where I kept my four pit bulls. This dog room was also the room where I stashed my money because I knew no one in my family liked dealing with my dogs. I had one of those heavy-duty plastic briefcase safes that I kept in the ceiling, and that's where I hid my cash.

As Nightmare, Savo, and I sat in my basement getting high and laughing about an event that took place a few nights before, I counted $17,100 I had saved up. I took $15,000 to purchase the car I wanted, an all-white 2007 Ford Explorer Sport Trac, and I took another $1,000 out to re-up, and put the remaining $1,100 back in my safe into the ceiling. That same day the deal was made, and I was driving off the lot feeling better than I had ever felt. Nightmare had a new car as well; he was driving around one of those half-gas, half-electric cars. Having these new cars that we cherished, we got away from the habit of searching for enemies out of our own cars and would only use cars that we would rent from our clients. This truck would become my everyday transportation. I had my whole family in this truck at one point in time or another.

Approximately six months passed by before I finally got pulled over by the police, which I wasn't worried about because I didn't have a gun with me at the time and the amount of crack I had was enough to swallow. As usual, I figured I would get a ticket for not having a license and be on my way, but after a second police car arrived, I knew it wasn't a good sign. Next thing I knew guns were being drawn, and I was taken from the car, put in cuffs, and read my rights. I was informed that the truck was stolen and had been taken for a test drive and never returned. I couldn't do anything but laugh at the fact that I got played for $15,000. That night, November 15, 2007, I was arrested for possession of a stolen vehicle. After spending the weekend in jail, it was time to go before the judge and make my argument. I explained to a lawyer that I had never known the car wasn't stolen. I had the keys and paperwork showing that I had permission to drive the car. After hearing the case, the judge dropped the charges to possession of stolen property, and I was released to my mom and given another court date. Of course I didn't show up for the next court hearing. On March 7, 2008, I was arrested once again for failure to appear or comply, and I was placed in DCYC.

While I was in DCYC, I became close with a guard. I believe the fact that I had an old-soul vibe, was young and humble, and was respected by my peers drew the guard close to me. I later learned that he enjoyed popping pills but had no way of getting them. This would be around the time pills were introduced to Omaha in the triple-stack form. He approached me about getting some, and I replied with an offer. We agreed that on every outside meal he let me order, I would give him two pills. I would usually order Burger King or Sonic, placing three pills between the sandwich; of course I needed a pill for myself. Nightmare or Savo would usually drop off the food, and this became an every-night routine.

On March 16, 2008, this guard came to my door with a look on his face that signaled there was a problem.

"La'Ron, I got to tell you something!"

"What's Groovie?" I asked, thinking that he might be having second thoughts about our deal.

"Your brother Jovan Reed [Nightmare] was just shot and killed by a police officer."

I was hurt! I felt my heart stop, and my eyes watered up. I slammed my cell door shut and cried for hours. At this point in my life, I had never lost a friend to gun violence. I was seventeen years old, sitting in a cage, and I must say it was a lot for me to process. The one person I looked up to was now dead. From that moment forward, I would forever view the police as my enemy. These same gang unit officers that killed him would always hop out on us, threating us, holding us at gun point, roughing us up, illegally searching us and our cars. From the jump, there was no way I thought it was justifiable. Shortly after, I learned that nightmare was shot in the back. I've had millions of conversations with Nightmare, and one thing that never crossed either of our minds was shooting at the police. The plan was always the same: the person who's riding with the gun sits by the door, and if the police gets behind us and hits the lights, you run. I guess on that day they didn't feel like chasing him or was tired of the fact that they could never catch us on feet.

I now 100-percent understood how it felt to be depressed. Everyone outside of our neighborhood really thought Nightmare and I were brothers because of how close we were. This very thought got me approved to attend his funeral. I remember waking up that day feeling a little better about myself because of the fact that I was going to the funeral to say my final goodbye. After about twenty minutes of sitting in the church parking lot, I was told that there were too many people attending and that I wouldn't be allowed to go inside. In my mind it was like he died all over again. I had to revisit all those feelings I had when I first heard that he had died. I once again found myself crying uncontrollably on the whole ride back to DCYC.

On April 11, 2008, I was released from DCYC, not really knowing what my plan was. As the saying goes, my life went from sugar to dookie. I had just taken a $15,000 loss, and I forgot to mention that after I was released for the truck, the police raided my house a few weeks later. They didn't find drugs but confiscated the $1,100 I had in the ceiling. My best friend with the connection died, so I had no way to re-up. I had left my trap phone with a female I was dating at the time, and she basically ran off with all my clients. So I was fresh out with no crack, no money, no gun, and really no secure place to live.

Lucky me, I had an ace in the hold: a White girl named Jenna who I had been in an on-and-off relationship with since 2006. My young mind was telling me North Omaha was too hot and it was time for a major shift, so I decided to move to La Vista, Nebraska, with Jenna in her mom's house. La Vista was about thirty minutes away from North Omaha, depending on the traffic. This transition was a perfect move for me at the right time. Also around this time, I made my mind up that I would only drive cars that had tinted windows. This allowed me to move in and out of Omaha without being noticed, which in turn allowed me to focus more on getting money and less on my enemies. Everything was starting to move in the right direction, but mentally I was still going through it. Daily I would still find myself stressing about life, having problems at Jenna's family's house, having problems in the streets, and the worse one of them all, a new fear was starting to form in my head about dying, not only from other gangs but also by the police.

Jenna's mom was cool with me being in her house, but her dad didn't feel the same way. Even though her dad didn't live there, his word still carried weight in their household. So one day while I was with Jenna, her dad called and asked to speak with me. Out the blue he started calling me all kinds of racist names, including the N bomb. He continued on threatening me and telling me that I had to leave their house, or he was going to come over and do this and that to me. And honestly, I wasn't concerned about his threats because if push comes to shove I wasn't fighting. Even worse, he mentioned that he was going to call the police to Jenna's house. This was a risk I wasn't willing to take. Nervous and paranoid, that same week I moved out.

I had been filling back up that same safe that the police had emptied out while I was living with Jenna. My first move was getting transportation. I purchased a 1964 Plymouth and took my show on the road. One of my clients at the time was a retired schoolteacher who lived a pretty stable life outside of getting high on the weekends. I told her about my situation on how I was pretty much homeless but could afford a place to stay if I found someone to put a place in their name for me. She agreed to do so if I paid the deposit and rent every month, and gave her a gram a week. I found a nice low-key apartment off Thirty-Fifth and Davenport Street and made that my home for the next year.

As I was maintaining and keeping a roof over my head, I continued to find myself trying to address most situations that were going on in my neighborhood. Even though I didn't live in the hood, you could catch me there on a daily in the middle or at the forefront of everything that was going on, whether it was friendships being broken behind money or envy, guns being stolen from hiding spots, cars and houses being shot up, fronting sacks and guys not paying their debts, running snitches out the neighborhood, or homies beefing with homies. One thing was clear: there was starting to be a division in our neighborhood. Lines were being drawn, and conversations were being had about one group being Thirty-Seventh Street Death Valley Crips and another being Thirty-Seventh Street Hoova Crips. Most of the young guys, including myself, represented Hoova Crips. And with this came the first time I would experience a homie shooting a homie. Blue didn't die, but the next day I found myself kicking down one of the older homies' door, named Cartoon, holding him at gunpoint with Mr. Woody looking for answers on the whereabouts of the person who shot Blue. Now not only were we watching out from guys from other neighborhoods, we also had to watch out for a handful of guys who felt they had the rights to run the same turf.

During these traumatic times of 2008, I also lost two other day-one friends from Hoovas. On July 3, 2008, my friend No-No was killed. No-No used to live with me when my mom stayed off Forty-Fifth and Bedford Street. On December 28, 2008, my friend Blue was killed in a robbery gone bad. Blue was one of the first guys I met from Hoovas. Also during these traumatic times, on July 7, 2008, my son, Kingzton Jones, was born. I remember it was a windy July night. I was riding around the city with my gun in my lap, making money moves, when I got the call that Keyana was about to have my son.

I rushed to the hospital, and thank God I made it on time because being a part of this experience has been the proudest moment of my life.

Once I entered the room, I grabbed a chair and sat in the corner. I instantly felt myself starting to sweat at the sight of Keyana laying there with her legs wide open. As I was watching from a distance, listening to her and the doctor converse on when to push and take a deep breath, along with her mom saying that she was doing a good job, I noticed a head starting to pop out. From that moment forward, I spaced off. I was visualizing the many drug transactions I had with my mom. It was that very moment that I realized not only was I destroying my mom's life, but if I continued our dealings I would be harming my son by him not being able to have the relationship with his grandma that I had with mine.

"La'Ron, La'Ron, La'Ron," Keyana's mom said, snapping me out of my thought.

"Yeah, what's up?" I replied.

"Do you want to cut the umbilical cord?"

"Of course!"

"Get up and come cut it. You're sweating like you're having the baby," she said, making everyone in the hospital room laugh.

As I started to cut the cord, the doctor showed me where to cut and told me not to be nervous. I was officially a father. From that moment forward, I stopped selling my mom drugs. Also, I felt like I had to change some things in my life to be the father I never had. Of course, it didn't change the fact that I still saw Akeem as my little brother. I would still come to the neighborhood and hang around the guys, pop bottles, show up for parties, hood meetings, etc. Akeem and I didn't always agree, but we knew what each other expected without having to communicate. But at the end of the day, we always had an understanding and respected each other's personal choices. But one thing I didn't think Akeem liked was how I was staring to shift away from gangbanging and more toward hustling.

The problem was I wasn't really sure what change looked like for me. The examples I had seen when it came to change were guys in the neighborhood that no longer gangbanged but still condoned in all sorts of illegal street hustles. As for me, that's what changing my life looked like as well. I was no longer spending my days in the hood waiting on my phone to ring to go get some money, which oftentimes would result in shootouts. I now ventured out to a trap house on Twenty-Fifth and Parker Street. This was a perfect location due to this area being in the middle of a slew of low-income houses, a homeless shelter, a street where all the prostitutes took their daily walk, and far enough from my neighborhood that no one would ever think to look for me there. But in my life story, there was still one problem. I opened the door to some of the same guys that I told myself I was getting away from. I guess in that moment I didn't realize change also meant leaving them behind.

For months, everything was running smooth. The trap house was running like a Rolex. I was getting more than I was making, sitting in the neighborhood and answering calls. I had my lady friend drop off my sacks, sometimes multiple times a day, and she picked up the money at the end of the night. This worked well for me because I didn't have to worry about having too much in the house at one time. On average, there were three or four guys hustling out this trap house, and we all were making enough money to provide for our families. There was no face-to-face transaction; a customer could only get served through the back window. There were nights when there was literally a line of cars outside, and we had to hire other crackheads to control the movement. The scene was similar to your local after-hour spot once the club closed.

It took a minute for the police to catch on, and once they did, they would constantly ride by the house real slow, so we knew it was only a matter of time before they kick the door in. To no surprise, that's what happened. Unfortunately for them, this would be the second time they raided a house with my name on the search warrant, but no La'Ron in sight. By the time the raid took place, I had already switched trap houses and set up shop at an apartment complex on Forty-Fifth and Hamilton Street that a few young guys controlled. It was more for me to have a place to sit because I was back only hustling off my phone. The house on Twenty-Fifth Street was shut down for business after the raid, but I still stopped by to visit my Whitebread homegirl who had rented the place.

A few weeks after the move, I made a play for $5,600. Once again. I was never the one to believe that you should have all your products in the trap house, but since that's where the deal was made at, I had no other choice. But there were also other problems. One, may I remind you that I never drove with more drugs than I could swallow. Two, I didn't have a driver's license. Three, I had a gun on me everywhere I went around this time. And the main problem was my homegirl, who would usually move the product, was at work. But one thing was for sure, I knew the product needed to be moved from Hamilton Street as soon as possible.

Akeem had a house he was living in about five minutes away. There was no illegal activity going on at his location, so I decided to take the risk and drive there to drop off the sack, while I go put my gun up and switch cars because the police knew my car as well. This would take me approximately thirty minutes.

When I entered Akeem's spot, as usual he was surrounded by his crew and a few mutual female friends we had. I told Akeem that I was going to switch cars and that I would be right back. About fifteen minutes after leaving his place my phone rang, and it was Akeem calling. I was hoping that what I heard on the other line of the phone was a joke. Somebody had just stolen my sack! I always get the question "You and Akeem used to be inseparable, what happened?" from people who knew Akeem and me in our younger days. Well, there's your answer.

This was the moment that changed the dynamic of our brotherly bond forever. Even though I didn't fall out with Akeem behind my sack being stolen because he never had possession, and I just left it where I left it inside our mutual friend's house. From that day forward, the trust was no longer there, at least on my end. The story I was told was that one of the females in the house had called up one of her relatives and mentioned what they had just seen. Due to the fact that this individual was related to the females whose house it was, he walked in and out without being questioned or searched. At this point in my life, I had never been robbed. Within that first week, I had been shot—the bullet hit my right wrist and came out my pinky. Also, during these traumatic times, I was interrogated for a murder, which became confusing because this wasn't the guy I had known to be responsible for taking my sack or being connected in any kind of way. The record reflects that I was in the hospital at the time, and I had metal rods in my dominant hand, so they knew it couldn't have been me who committed the murder.

Also during the these traumatic times on March 8, 2009, in a separate incident one of my day-one friends, Arius Devers, a.k.a. E-Bo, was shot and pronounced dead due to a gunshot wound to the head. As I was dealing with life and all these emotions I was feeling while lying in the hospital, I realized that there was no one there for me emotionally but Jenna. The reality was people were either mad at me or scared to be around me.

I was still trying to bounce back from the $15,000 I lost, on top of the $1,100 the police took from my dog room out the ceiling, on top of being set back another $5,600. As I mentioned earlier, street wars are not cheap, especially when you're playing for keeps. Of course I was low on cash again. The trap house on Hamilton had been shot up during these weeks of shootings, and one of my cars was shot up. May I remind you that I was eighteen years old at this time; mentally this was a lot to handle.

After the shootings calmed down, I found myself debating on what would be my next money move. My best option was to open the trap house back up on Twenty-Fifth and Parker Street. Of course I knew this was a bad idea, but this was guaranteed fast money. Desperate times call for desperate measures. Plus, I now had these medal rods in my right hand to heal my bones back in place, so if something was to happen, there was no way I could shoot first or shoot back. I had to lay low. And in no time, the trap house was back running like a Rolex.

On April 9, 2009, I went to my favorite BBQ spot, Jim's Rib Haven, to get something to eat before I started my long day at the trap house. As soon as I got to Parker Street, I had a feeling that something wasn't right. Once I entered the back door I heard a loud boom, followed by the sound of glass shattering. My first thought was *Here we go again, another shootout*. But after I didn't hear a second shot, I knew what time it was. The police had shot a bean bag through the window, and "Police Department" was starting to be echoed all throughout the house. They made sure they didn't miss me this time. The search ended with them finding 3.4 grams of crack and two guns. Even though the house wasn't in my name, I was charged with what they had found in the house due to my name being on pill bottles prescribed for my injury. I was arrested and taken to the county jail, where I received a bond. Jenna came to pick me up that same night. The gun charges were dismissed due to I not being in the vicinity of where they were found, and I was convicted to a few months in the county jail for the crack even though I wasn't in the vicinity of where they found that either. This was my first time doing county jail time.

At this point, it seemed impossible to get ahead. I was taking loss after loss, my neighborhood was beefing with three different gangs, so I was back in the position where I was trying to gangbang and hustle at the same time. If you're from the streets, you know it's hard to do both. A group of guys from Hoovas decided to go to a new club that had just open in South Omaha. It seemed as if the South Family guys knew they were coming. Before they made it in the club an altercation broke out, and Maxxo was shot and killed at the club entrance. This became phase two of another multigenerational beef. Here's an ironic story. The guy Bernard "Nardo" Long, who I spoke about being someone who I looked up to from the stories I heard about him, was convicted of killing a guy from South Family Projects, named Maxx. Now years later, our friend Maxxo was killed by the South Project gang. How ironic!

Loss after loss, friend after friend, how does a nineteen-year-old young man cope? Regardless of how much money I was getting in the streets or how much work I was putting in for my neighborhood, I found myself going through it mentally, isolating myself, and the trust issues I had been dealing with for years were now turning into paranoia. During this time of isolation, I noticed another bad habit starting to form. I was drinking liquor more than I ever had. At the time, I didn't look at it as having an alcohol problem, mainly because

I could afford what I was drinking. I went from being a social drinker to drinking two or three pints by myself a day. Even though I didn't express or know how to express that I was struggling mentally, I realized that I was losing myself in the street life and needed to do something about it. In my young mind, I had tried everything I possibly could to survive these mean streets of North Omaha. I had reached a dead end, and there was only one place left for me to go for love, support, stability, comfort, and a peace of mind: Mama's house. For years I tried to keep the street life away from my family's house, and I would say I did a great job due to the fact that my mom's house had never been shot up.

Regardless of going back to my mom's house, I was still battling with my demons. And the sad part was that no one in my house even noticed; to them this was normal La'Ron, a person that I had grown to be. The first thing I did was put up a surveillance camera to watch the backdoor which led straight to the basement where I slept. At this time, I was carrying around a hand cannon. Within the first week of moving back into my mom's house, I found myself contemplating suicide. I went as far as putting one bullet in the gun and spinning the barrel, taking a large gulp of Hennessy, and telling myself that this was my destiny. Outside of the blood that's been spilt in the streets, my main two thoughts were, I would rather kill myself before the streets do and that if I did this I was going to go out like my father, one to the head. Those thoughts were interrupted by a voice that I heard speak to me clearly, "I'm not done with you!" I never raised the magnum to my temple.

Like all my rock-bottom moments, I realized that it was time to come up with a new game plan. One thing was for sure, I had to really follow through with creating distance from the younger guys that were coming up in the hood. I was once again done with hustling out a trap house and only hustled off my phones. I, for sure, didn't have my clients come to my mom's house because I understood how that first raid I put my family through on Bedford Street—with the police rushing in, guns being drawn on them, and police making my family lay on the floor—was a traumatic experience. I wasn't willing to put them through that again. I still had my 1967 Plymouth that I wasn't driving, so I made this car my new stash spot. This way I didn't have to worry about nothing coming up missing or the police confiscating my money in a raid. This worked well for me because I was able to move the car from trusted clients to clients' houses, keeping them in the dark by telling them I needed to keep the car there until I sold it. Once again, I was back on track hustling hard and saving money.

Soon after, I moved out of my mom's house. Jenna and I got our first apartment together off Sixtieth and Center Street, well away from North Omaha. A short period of time after I purchased a 1978 Buick Regal Turbo Coupe for $2,500, I spent another $3,500 on chrome door handles and trimmings, and a 7 Up (soda) candy-green paint job which symbolizes the seven in Thirty-Seventh Street. I also added a TV deck, speakers, and a white leather rag top which cost about another $1,000. Money spent, money gone. In the streets this was what we call *hustling backward*—when you save up money just to spend it on materialistic things. By the end of 2009, everywhere I went people seemed to know who I was or had at least heard about me. The street reality was that I had earned some street respect that had reached outside of my neighborhood and my guys. I had survived my BG days and had reached YG status, so for me, putting this car together on my own, all off street money, was a way to show my success; it was my trophy. This was another moment I felt like I had honored my gang and improved my street reputation. It's rare within the corners of North Omaha to see a nineteen-year-old young man, who wasn't spoon-fed, riding around shining how I was, hustling and gangbanging.

In my younger years I was known for setting street standards. I had put in the work in my younger days and would continue to do so if someone crossed the line. I fought the court system without snitching on my friends, taught numerous guys in my hood the means to provide for their family. I was known for always having a gun. I always kept one of the baddest females who had her own. I had that dope boy swag. I wore a lot of gold jewelry: three rings on my left hand, a Cuban link chain with a C medallion, and a pair of square cannery yellow diamond earrings. For me, the biggest thing was I didn't mind supporting my guys financially. I was what the streets would refer to as an all-around street dude—real n*gga. But there was one area that I had always fell short in. Since my Miami Park days, I never had my own connection. But this was about to change.

In 2010, I was riding around the city, making money moves. So not only was I making a name for myself when it came to gangbanging, I was also known as a youngster with a nice hustle. That same year I was connected with an older guy who I had known from my younger days. I would see him from time to time as a youngster riding all types of ATVs and driving nice cars. Growing up, I always heard that this guy was a drug dealer and a troublemaker. But regardless, all the kids in the neighborhood admired him. We loved to watch as he would come down the block on his ATVs popping wheelies from one corner to the next. Now years later I was connected to this very guy I grew up admiring. How was that for a coincidence, right? But what was about to come with this was totally unexpected and would only heighten my paranoia.

I learned that the biggest misconceptions people had was that I personally had a lot of money and drugs. Of course this was what I was projecting. I was driving a nice car, stayed dressed up, but personally I was still dealing with my alcoholism. Literally, in every club I went to I would spend no less than $100 on bottles which became a regular weekend thing to do that summer. On many occasions a few of the neighborhood hustlers, including a few from other neighborhoods that we were cool with, would pull out our cars and ride around the city with more than ten cars in a row. I mean 2010 was the year of stunting which comes with a price tag, on top of managing my own life, bills, needs, and wants. But with everything I was projecting in the streets came envy and a handful of my guys in my neighborhood who felt like I should have been looking out for them as well. Now the word was going around that some guys from my neighborhood had plans to rob me, and the sad part was my young guy Savo was at the forefront of this conversation.

Savo was Nightmare's younger cousin and righthand man. After Nightmare died, I and Savo became a lot closer. He became my new partner in crime; there were many nights of just he and I riding around the city with guns up to no good. This was someone that I had semi-trusted, and anytime that I needed him he was always there, vice versa. It added fuel to the fire when word got around that I was fronting Milton drugs, which wasn't true. Milton had been in Omaha for some time now, but due to the fact that he didn't gang-bang, he was able to fly under the radar. Savo and a handful of others never liked Milton mainly because I was always protecting him. Savo and I reached our last straw the day he finally ran across Milton and I, sitting outside some apartment buildings. Savo was in the car with two other guys from Hoovas, Penny and J7. So once Savo spotted my car, he hopped out his car with no hesitation, and so did I with my gun in hand. To my surprise, Savo didn't have his gun, but he insisted that I had to let him fight Milton since he had heard that Milton has been running his mouth about Savo and I's situation. Of course Savo ran up on Milton, and Milton got to running around my car from Savo, saying that he didn't want to fight. I told Savo that I wasn't going to make Milton fight, and if he touched Milton, I was going to shoot him in the leg. Savo was mad. He talked about how he always had my back, and even worse, he said that he was going to get his gun and that he was going to be looking for me. Even though I had the upper hand, I let him go. But one thing was for sure, I didn't take his threat lightly. I knew he was dangerous. But overall, I really did have love and the utmost respect for Savo and couldn't see myself harming him. I never believed in homies beefing with homies. But at the same time I have been protecting Milton since we were kids, and I wouldn't turn my back on Milton for anyone.

 Savo and I ran across each other a few days after, and we put the guns down and fought like men. The last time I spoke to Savo, I was sitting at Tatianna's apartment with my older homie Cin-Locc when Savo called his phone and asked to speak with me. After hearing each other out, we agreed that it was all love and that we would stay out of each other's way. I remember both of our last words.

 "You know I love you, Savo," I said.

 "I love you too, but you are not the same person!" he replied.

 On November 7, 2010, less than a week after we talked, I got the call that he and Penny had been gunned down during a drug deal. He had started buying dope from some guys from a different neighborhood and was set up. Furthermore, I was hurt and back in the streets trying to revenge their deaths. I couldn't win for losing!

Since my introduction to the gang life, I had lost nine close friends from Hoovas and four other associates. By this time I had been shot four times, each time on separate occasions. I had lost so much money, I lost count. I remember on many occasions evaluating my life and not understanding why God would allow me to experience so much death, heartaches, stress, depression, pain, hurt, adversity, and overall the day-to-day paranoia and anxiety of a wanted man doing what he had to in order to stay alive. Honestly, I couldn't even begin to guess how many shootouts I have been in. My old enemies would say that I was "hard to kill," but I would say since an itty bitty kiddy I've been praying to God. I would always tell my guys that I'm blessed! That's how I truly felt, like God had sent someone to watch over me. Maybe it was my dad, Timothy; my grandma, Essie; Nightmare, or God himself. Whoever it was did an excellent job. Would you agree?

REVIEW BOOK CLUB QUESTIONS.

Post-Traumatic Street Disorder

Left to Right, Top to bottom…
Blue, Nightmare, Savo, Penny
Maxxo, Ebo, NoNo
Savo, Nightmare

CHAPTER 8

Warning Signs

By the end of 2010, I began to notice many different warning signs appear in my life that I would ignorantly ignore. But now I sit in this cell, finding myself often reflecting on these moments and their meaning. I must say now I understand what God was trying to show me.

* * * * *

Shortly after Savo and Penny died, I was sitting at Tatianna apartment with Locc when I got an alarming phone call. This call consisted of two guys who I knew, and I felt there was a very high chance that they knew who was responsible for Savo and Penny's death. Within minutes Locc and I were standing at their car door with gun in hand. I knew one of the guys was a major coke head, and by all the information he was giving me, I knew he had to be high. I didn't know what came over me, but I told Locc let's go. The look on Locc's face screamed confusion and disappointment. Years later, I talked to Locc about this day, and I knew him not pulling the trigger that night has been something he always regretted. We had the chance to get even, and I went against the grain. Why is this story important? Anybody who know me personally would tell you that I had a good heart and always looked out for others. But in the gang culture there is a belief that you don't let your enemies slide if

Warning Signs

you have the upper hand. Was this the first major break in my life of the battle between La'Ron versus Clown? Whatever God was trying to show me, one thing is for sure, I kept ignoring the signs.

On August 8, 2011, I got a call from some Hoova Crips who were having a BBQ and wanted me to show up. This wasn't out of the ordinary. If I was there, for sure we would have plenty of liquor to drink. Plus, I would often find myself clowning, being the life of the party, which was fun for everyone around me. As I was there enjoying myself, having a good time, I noticed a crackhead, who would later be identified as Mr. Valentines, walk by wearing a light blue number-7 FUBU jersey. Another fact about me: if you know me, then you know there's not too much more I love doing than spending time with crackheads. Majority of my customers were like family to me and had been around for years. But occasionally, I would run across street walkers that didn't have any money who were willing to try almost anything I dared them to or perform a talent that they had before their addiction, such as boxing, singing, rapping, making jokes, and dancing. Even a few didn't mind cleaning my car, dog kennel, or a trap house. Mr. Valentine was a new face I had never seen around the neighborhood, and my first thought was that he could possibly be a new customer. He approached me next to a car I was standing by that I had intentionally parked sideways. In case someone did a drive by, I would have coverage.

"A young brother let me hold a couple dollars," he asked me, initiating the conversation.

"Let me buy that jersey from you. Seven is my lucky number," I replied.

"Nah, I don't believe in selling the clothes off my back. Do you have some stuff?

"What type of question is that? Are you the police?" I asked.

"Nah, I'm not the police. I live up the street. Do you want to see my ID?" he asked.

"Now you're trying to get my fingerprints too," I said, smiling but still thinking that he was acting a little suspicious. "I'll take your word for it. I'm C, by the way," I said, giving him my hustle name.

"All right, C."

"Where are you headed?" I asked.

"I'm going to the store and buy me a drink. Let me hold $5, and I'll wash your car when I get back."

"Who said this was my car?" I asked, still suspicious.

"Well, I'll wash all these cars out here," he said, laughing.

"How about you just sell me your FUBU jersey for $5?"

"Nah, C, I can't do that."

"Do you have any hidden talents?" I asked.

"Hell yeah, I used to be one of the best singers back in my days. What you want to hear, C?"

"Sing me some Keith Sweat. Let me see what you got!"

After about a good minute listening to Mr. Valentines sing, remixing a song by Keith Sweat, repeating the same verse. He said, "I will sell you, my jersey."

"I was just joking. I don't want—"

The next thing I recall was hearing God speak to me, "Get up, I'm not done with you." Not only did I hear him, but as I was getting off the ground it felt as if someone was picking me up by my shirt. As I got up confused, I instantly noticed the blood stain on my shirt and realized that I had been shot in the stomach. Even worse, I also noticed Mr. Valentines laying lifeless in front of me on the ground, eyes shut. I knew he was dead. I immediately jumped in the car and started to drive myself to the hospital. As I was driving and holding the rag tightly to my stomach, I could feel myself blacking in and out, fighting for my life. My guys noticed it as well, and one of them decided to switch me seats and take over the wheel. As I was replaying what just happened in my head, I could not recall hearing one gunshot, so the first bullet must have hit me. I was thinking about the words I heard God speak to me and praying that I didn't die.

As we pulled up to the emergency door, I hopped out and they drove off. As soon as my foot hit the entrance, I passed out again. I woke up chained to a bed, and if I remember correctly, my mom, Jenna, and some detectives were at my bed side. As I was lying in the hospital, I kept receiving messages that the rumor was that I had died, but once again I pulled through. This was my fifth time getting shot. I spent two weeks in the hospital recovering before I was able to leave. When I got out Akeem was the first person to come visit me and see how I was doing. I had lost at least twenty pounds. I couldn't stand up straight, and my body was stuck in a 70-degree angle. I had two different fluid bags coming out of my stomach, I could barely eat, and my stomach had been stapled and wasn't fully healed from the surgery, so you could literally see into my stomach. Once again, it was time to lay low, which I did for about two months, moving from house to house. One thing was for sure, I wasn't in shape for war.

On top of the physical pain I was feeling, I was also informed that one of the other Hoova guys had been shot. But thank God he was wearing a bulletproof vest. For those few months I spent healing, I couldn't get my mind off Mr. Valentines, but selfishly I couldn't help but think how that number-seven jersey had been a big factor into saving my life. Seven has always been a significant number in my life that always seemed to manifest itself. For example, my grandma had seven kids, my mom was born on March 7, I was born on March 27, my sister Pra'Shae was born on April 17, my son was born on July 7 (seventh month, seventh day), and the gang I claimed was Thirty-Seventh Street. And not only did the number seven show up through people in my life, it also manifested itself in a negative way. I was charged with the first murder on January 7 and the second murder on March 7. Was the seven on Mr. Valentines's jersey another warning sign on what was about to take place on January 7, 2013, and March 7, 2014?

Months had passed since the shooting took place, and I was finally moving around the city again. During this time I met the woman I once referred to as my soul mate, Millini, whose birthday just happened to have a seven in it, December 27. There has been a handful of women who I can say I truly loved: Keke, Jenna, Keyana, Tatianna, and now Millini. I admired Millini's loyalty, her strength as a Black woman, and most importantly, how she managed to raise three kids on her own, just as my mom did with me and my two younger sisters. When I first laid my eyes on Millini, I remember telling myself that I had to have her. I even remember the corny pick-up line I used in my attempt to do so, which must have had some kind of effect because over time we would always laugh about it. The pick-up line was meant to compliment her native look. "Damn,

Pocahontas, where have you been all my life? I've been looking for you!" And I said it with so much swag and confidence. Everybody in the house laughed at me, and she immediately shut me down. Stop playing, you know I wasn't going to let her get away! In less than a month, I had her riding shotgun around the city with me. She would also become the first woman I dated that I could honestly see myself marrying. Unfortunately for Millini, we met at a time when I didn't understand how to master my post-traumatic street disorder and when my life was slowly spiraling down the drain, along with my hustle, my womanizing, and my alcoholism. Furthermore, just like Tatianna, Millini knew about Jenna and accepted the fact that she was my number one. Even though they were never friends, they got to the point where they began to communicate and accepted the fact that I would bounce from house to house. When you're living the street life, it really doesn't get too much better than having your women on the same page.

New love, new energy, but financially I was still at a standstill. For some time now, I had been disconnected with my connect, which I'm sure he realized that I was drawing too much heat to myself. I still had my 1978 Regal put away in my mom's garage that I would rarely drive due to the police always harassing me. They kept pulling me over giving me ticket after tickets, until I was finally revoked and sentenced to five months in jail. While in the county jail I told myself that I couldn't keep giving them the upper hand and I had to get my driver's license. After getting out of jail I would study for my driving license test. But in between time, the first of the month through the fifteenth, when the government checks came out, I still had to have someone drive me around in the Regal. Even though I always kept my gun, I must admit I never seemed to be at ease with whoever was driving me around. The last thing I needed was another death on my conscience.

I was always looking for a solution, and I had a habit of switching cars through the week to keep my enemies and the police guessing. I also relied on my clients to rent me their cars. I had a client who worked at H&H who would let me rent his car (different guy from the one who sold me the boggish truck). I had another client who was a high school football coach and had a nice red Chevy pickup truck that I rented. That truck got me through the winter, but renting cars can be expensive, so this was not a habit I was willing to get used to. As soon as the winter was over, I went to take my driver's license test, and I failed. I went back to take it a few weeks later, and I passed. For me, this only meant that I had a license to drive with my gun. But even with my license, I had no interest in driving around the city in my Regal. My guy from Hoovas, named Tenn, owned a 1994 Chevy Blazer, and I had decided to trade him the Regal for his truck, which I took as a loss. There were two factors I was sold on. One, Tenn didn't gangbang, so I didn't have to worry about anybody trying to shoot the truck up. Two, all my cars in the past had hidden compartments where I could hide my gun, and so did this truck. Regardless of me routinely switching cars, there was one thing that would remain the same: my fear of death, which wouldn't allow me to stop riding with a gun. Was this another warning sign?

One night, as I was riding around the city with Jenna, I got a call from a client that lived on the west side of town, which is not known to be a high-crime area. Like I would do on any other day, I pulled into the one-way apartment and parked in front of their door. Seconds later, I noticed a police car pulling up behind me with their lights off. Two White police officers immediately got out their car, guns drawn, one approaching the driver's side and the other on the passenger side. Once again, I had a stash spot in the truck where I could hide my gun, but they pulled up so quick I wasn't able to make my move. So I just threw my gun under the seat and raised my hand per their request.

"Roll your window down!" the officer demanded.

"What's the problem, Officer?" I asked after rolling my window down.

"Let me see some identification."

"No problem, Officer, here's my license, registration, and proof of insurance."

"I'm going to need you to step out of the car. Do you have anything in here I should be worried about?" he asked without even running my name through the system.

"Yes, Officer, I have a gun under my seat."

"Okay, do as I tell you. Turn off your engine, take the keys out and put them on the dash, put your hands back up in the air, and don't move."

The officer now had his gun drawn, and his barrel was staring me right in the eye. I was arrested and charged with possession of a firearm, and my bail was set at 10 percent of $25,000. Jenna came to bail me out that same night.

At this point in my life, I had never been to prison, but I had just been caught red-handed with a gun, so I was worried that my streak would soon be over and I could be on my way to the big house. On the other hand, I understood my Fourth Amendment Rights, and I knew the police officers had no probable cause to search my truck. Regardless of my legal situation, I was down $2,500 and my bills still had to be paid. So I was back on my regular routine, riding around with a sack and my gun managing my life the only way I knew how. Still staying on track, not partying, I wasn't in the hood and I was still switching cars like I owned a dealership. But I just caught a charge in my truck, so I felt like it was time to switch my personal car again. I knew a guy who owned a 1986 Monte Carlo SS. It was smoke gray with the black grill, with smoke-gray-black-and-red interior. The SS ran but needed some engine work. I had put off getting the car during the winter, but now it was warming up. It was time to make the call. The other issue I had was that this car didn't have tint. I could have easily put tent on there, but I was a firm believer that certain cars shouldn't be tampered with. For me this was one of those cars. Millini liked the truck and we would switch cars from time to time, so before I made the trade I wanted her opinion. She really didn't care but insisted that she did like the SS, especially since she had an ash gray 2008 Chevy Impala SS. So essentially we had his and her SS's.

Outside of the new case, everything in my life had been going well. I hadn't been in a shootout in months. I was also starting to spend more time with Kingzton. During Keyana's pregnancy, I had all these ideas on what being a dad looked like and being the dad for Kingzton I never had. But being a cheater and a womanizer and trying to make every woman I dated happy tainted my vision on what I once saw myself as when it came to being a father. It is sad, but I am just being honest.

When Kingzton was born, I was in a relationship with Jenna. She got pregnant before Keyana, but Jenna decided to have an abortion. It was Jenna's choice and a choice that I respected because ultimately I believe a woman should always own the right to choose what she does with her body. But looking back, what I didn't realize was the trauma that it would create for her until Kingzton was born and how every time she saw me with Kingzton it reminded her of her abortion and unborn child. Before Jenna and I had our own apartment, there were many days I would stop by Keyana's mom's house and spend time with them in their driveway, mainly because I never felt comfortable being around Keyana's family. My mom would always get Kingzton on the weekend, so I would spend time with him there as well. I thought all that would change when Jenna and I got our first apartment, but it didn't. Every time I would bring Kingzton around Jenna, I saw a different side of her. Her whole attitude would change. She was struggling in a way that I didn't fully understand at the time. But at the same time, she failed to realize that I was struggling to be a dad as well. Millini, on the other hand, accepted Kingzton, and she didn't mind me bringing him to her house. So in that way, Millini assisted me in becoming a better father. I started to pick Kingzton up from school every day. I got us both gym memberships so we could go play basketball together or so he could watch me play with other guys. In a matter of months, I felt that I was making improvements in my fatherhood; plus, there was still a chance that I could be going to prison soon, so I wanted to spend as much time with Kingzton as possible. I was enjoying every minute of it. These days made me realize what being a womanizer made me miss out on. This story is also important because this would be the first situation that made me feel like Jenna wasn't the one for me. Was this another warning sign?

I was out on bond juggling life, fatherhood, finances, relationships, alcoholism, my fear of death, and trying to stay alive. And on top of all that, I was getting closer and closer to my trial date. On January 6, 2013, I got a call from my lawyer, asking me to stop by her office so we could discuss our defense. I told her that I could be there tomorrow, on the seventh, and she gave me the time to be there and told me that she would be waiting. This wasn't unusual because I had been to her office before, and honestly I thought she had a crush on me. The last time we met, she had on a short skirt positioned so I could see between her legs. She had her shoes off showing all ten of her polished toes. Unusual, right? So the next day approached and Jenna drove me to my lawyer's office. For some strange reason, I had the weirdest feeling ever in my gut, similar to the feeling I had when I walked through the back door on Hamilton Street right before the police came rushing in. As we parked, I told Jenna that something didn't feel right. I put my gun in the glove box, gave her a kiss, and told her that I would be out as soon as possible. When I entered the building, I noticed two police officers checking me out from head to toe. Instantly after I made it through the metal detectors, the officers approached me.

"Are you La'Ron Jones?"

"Yes, sir, I am. Is there a problem, Officer?" I replied.

"We're going to need you to put your hands behind your back and cuff up. You have a warrant for first-degree murder."

In that moment I couldn't help but to giggle to myself knowing that I had just been set up by my lawyer. Entrapment? Was this the first warning sign that the county officials were out to get me by any means?

On the drive from my lawyer's office to the county jail, I was 100 percent confused as to what all this could be about. All the guys that I had gangbanged with in my BG days were dead, and I was never the type to brag about what I did or who I did it to. So the question remained: who was I accused of murdering? The next morning, I got a visit from my new two female lawyers who came with the information on who I was accused of murdering. Once they told me the name, it all made sense. "I'm innocent!" I had never met this guy I was accused of murdering in my life. I believe he was about ten years older than I was, and I would later find out that he was a Fortieth Avenue Crip OG, which is never good news when you're accused of murdering an OG who no longer gangbanged. Even though I was innocent, I still found myself dealing with guilt, questioning myself and God, thinking that this had to be my lot for all that I have done in the past. Another untrue rumor had been going around for years that I was the shot caller for the Hoova Crips and Akeem was my hitman. I'm sure the police thought the same as well. So I was also thinking maybe they put these false charges on me hoping that I would turn state on my neighborhood. The last thought I had was maybe the gun I was out on bail for came back dirty. But it couldn't have, because I bought it fresh out the box. One thing was for sure, whatever the case was, all I could really think was, in one way or another, I was in jail for a murder I didn't commit and how my past had an evil way of catching up to me. This was God's way of punishing me. Was this another warning sign as to what was going to happen in March 2014?

I soon found out the evidence that the state had against me was a statement a female made who was in or close by the car when the murder took place. Her statement was that she *heard*—emphasis on the *heard*—that it was a guy named La'Ron who did it. After being shown a photo lineup with my picture included, she pointed me out but told the police that she wasn't sure, and that was all it took for a twenty-two-year-old young man to be falsely arrested. My attorney who represented me for the gun case recused herself, so my new attorneys took over that case as well. From the jump, I liked the fact that they never came to me with a plea deal and insisted that we file a motion to cross-examine the two officers and to suppress the evidence. The day of the motion arrived, and both officers showed up to tell their side of the story on what led to my arrest. The issues my attorneys were addressing was there was no probable cause to jump out their car on me and that their actions was consistent with profiling—*racial* profiling. The first officer stated the reason he jumped out the car was he smelt marijuana when he pulled up behind my truck. He went on to say that once he approached my truck door, he asked me to roll the window down. The second officer stated nothing about marijuana but said he asked Jenna to roll her window down. The question then became, how did you smell marijuana when both of the truck windows were rolled up?

A few days later, I got a letter in the mail saying the case had been dismissed. One down and one to go.

I'm sure you could imagine the gun charge was the least of my worries. At this point in my life, the most time I had ever did behind bars was five months for reckless driving while being revoked. So coping with doing time was an everyday process. I am pretty good at poker, so I spent my days running a poker table and gambling on three-on-three basketball. But what helped me cope the most was Akeem was also in the county jail at this time, and he was my cellmate which made dealing with my emotions a lot easier. My three queens also played their role during this difficult time. Tatianna was always one phone call away and made sure I had mail coming in. Jenna came to visit once a week and would put $50 a week on my books even though I had my stash at her house. Millini came to visit from time to time and sent books, magazines, and personal photos that helped me decompress. So mentally it was hard, but emotionally I had a great support system.

After eight long months of this steady routine, I had only seen the judge once which was during my first month of being locked up. In September 2013, I was finally sitting in front of the judge again for a motion to suppress identification.

The female witness came inside the courtroom, and may I remind you that this was our first time seeing each other. She took a look at me and said, "I picked La'Ron out of the lineup, but I told the police that I wasn't sure" (paraphrased). After her statement and my attorneys making the argument on why this case should be dismissed and I should be released immediately, the judge agreed and even went on to apologize for what I had been through. I was transported back to the county jail to be booked out. But before I was able to leave, I had to go back to my unit to pack all my belongings. I gave Akeem everything I had except my books and mail and patiently waited on my name to be called. Within hours I was released, and Jenna was sitting in the parking lot waiting on me. To no surprise, the first thing I noticed was I was being watched. I spotted two guys sitting in a dark green trailblazer about a half block away watching me through binoculars. I had just been acquitted for a gun that I got caught red-handed with and a murder. I was sure the state and even the Feds were not happy.

But I failed to pay attention to the warning signs!

REVIEW BOOK CLUB QUESTIONS.

CHAPTER 9

The Fear of Death

As I was pulling out of the county jail's parking lot, past experiences of my life were flashing before my eyes: family, friends, women, drugs, money, betrayal, and murders. You would think a person that has been acquitted for murder would surely be thinking about their future. My negative recollection of my past was interrupted when Jenna passed me a Newport long cigarette that I don't recall passing back. As I cracked the car window to make way for the smoke to exit the vehicle, my attention was drawn to the trees in the near distance. For some odd reason, it seemed like the trees were bigger than I remembered. The grass seemed greener; it seemed as if everything around me had gotten a whole lot bigger. *But what else should you expect after living in a box for eight months?* I thought to myself.

My gaze went from the trees to the rearview mirror, and instantly after taking a look at a few cars behind me, my heart started to race, my palms started to sweat, and I felt like I was being followed. But it wasn't the feeling of being followed that had me paranoid because I had seen who I believed to be the Feds in the dark green Blazer watching me through binoculars. So I was sure they probably had a few cars following me and even waiting at my apartment. The paranoia stemmed from a thought that was real in my head and from my past experience. *What if someone decided to pull up beside me and start shooting and I didn't have a gun to shoot back? What if this guy I was accused of killing family was after me?* These were the thoughts I had as I felt myself get more paranoid by the second. A person on the outside looking in would say I was scared. But my life experience knew in a split second my thoughts could turn into a reality. In this moment I also realized I would now have a new set of enemies that I didn't know by name or face. As Jenna merged onto the interstate, my worries eased away as I got farther and farther away from North Omaha.

On the flip side of my fears was confusion. I wanted to change my life. While I was in the county jail, I told my family and friends that I would get out and do just that—change my life. But once again, I guess now the question was, what did change look like for me? After spending some much-needed time with Jenna, it was time to mentally formulate a plan. Getting out the county, all I had to my name was $3,500, a 1986 Monte Carlo SS, and a head full of ideas on what changing my life should look like.

The next day I woke up, ate breakfast, ironed my clothes, took a shower, and out the door I went to get my gun. With this gun in arm's reach, I was now feeling safe and ready to begin my homecoming tour around North Omaha, cautiously and prepared. But first, it was time for a slight change of wardrobe. I decided to go pick up Milton and take him on this adventure with me to the Westroads Mall. My normal attire was V-neck T-shirts, hoodies, cargo shorts, jeans, dickies with a variety of colors, Nike shoes, and Polo boots. For me, a part of this new change was also getting rid of this thuggish dope boy swag I was projecting. By the time Milton and I left the mall, I spent almost $2,000. I bought five different colors of 501 Levi jeans, five 8732 shirts (Young Jeezy clothing line), a new pair of Polo boots, a few hats, three watches that cost $100 each, and Hollister cologne. I also bought me, Milton, and Kingzton matching pairs of Nike shoes.

Afterward, I stopped by Millini's house to spend time with her and show my appreciation for staying by my side while I was in the county jail. The last stop was my mom's house so I could spend time with the family. I also had my SS in her garage, so I also had to meet the tow truck company so he could take my car to get a tune-up. While I was waiting on the tow truck company, Tatianna came over to see me, and of course I had to show her my appreciation as well for staying by my side during my county jail time. We had a good time on top of the SS. I also needed to have a conversation with my mom's husband, Mark, about helping me get a job. Mark was a supervisor at Omaha Paper Stocking Company. He assured me that he would help me get a job if I was committed to showing up for work. I talked with him about my experience fighting the murder case and how I felt like that was my wake-up call and that if he got me the job I wouldn't let him down. The next day I went to fill out the application, had an onsite interview, and was given a start date for the following Monday. At this point I was doing everything I had told my friends and family that I was going to do once I got out, and I was making it all come together one day at a time.

    Once again, on my street journey I often ran across OGs from various hoods who proclaimed they change their lives, in the sense that they were no longer gangbanging. But these same guys would still be in the hoods giving out hypocritical information. I saw that, been there, done that, and I felt like there was no way possible that I was going back to the street lifestyle. I felt that I had led the way in so many negative things, and now it was time to show my neighborhood what being a real OG was all about.

    Change for me always had that part attached with me telling myself that I had to stay away from the hood, but that never changed anything because my mentality and my love for the neighborhood kept me going back for more. Plus, there was a part of me that felt like I abandoned my neighborhood. But this time I wanted to take some guys with me on this journey. I got Akeem and his crew to start meeting me at the gym and local parks to work out or play basketball. Even though we still would be surrounded by a few guns, I was sure this was the most positive thing we had done for some time now. Change for me also looked like settling down with one woman. I moved out from Jenna and moved in with Millini to focus more on our relationship. Change for me looked like spending more time with Kingzton, so I was back picking him up from school daily and taking him to the gym with me on the weekends. Change for me looked like no longer smoking marijuana, so I quit after getting out of the county jail. And the biggest part of that change consisted of no longer selling drugs, so I hadn't touched a sack since leaving the county jail. Even though I was making some major adjustments in my life, my fear of death was always at the forefront of my mind. I couldn't imagine putting down my gun. In the words of my favorite rap artist, Boosie Badazz, "I stayed alive because I stayed strapped," which meant in my mind having a gun was the only thing that could keep me alive. I, for sure, didn't survive in the streets without having one.

But with any real change comes challenges. I started working and everything was going well. Of course, I was carrying my gun to work every day and soon started back dating multiple women, but outside of that my life had been a 337-degree turn around—short of 360 degrees, but a turnaround for sure.

After getting my second paycheck, I can recall this was the first time I felt discouraged. I was earning a little over $300 a week, and what happened next was an unexpected surprise. My check was a little over $150, and I soon found out that it didn't take child support long to collect their cut. So let's dissect the numbers. I was making between $300 to $350 a week; phone bill was $80 a month; car insurance in addition to SR22's was $270 a month; $25 for gas; $5 for a pack of cigarettes every morning, that's $900 a month; so in all, that's $1,250 I was putting out every month. After child support, I went from possibly making $1,200 to $1,400 a month to now making an average of $668 a month. The story of my life: I couldn't win for losing. And of course my initial thought was to buy me a sack and reconnect with my old clients. But truth be told, I really enjoyed the feeling of waking up and going to work and being able to cash a check at the end of the week. Even though I was battling with these thoughts and had to put out more money than I was making, I decided to keep my job and rely on my three queens for extra support. But there would soon be another problem: snow was in the near forecast. I knew my SS wouldn't be reliable in the snow, so my plans were to get a rental car for the winter. I had a homegirl named Latrice who had basically watched me grow up since my BG days. I believed she also enjoyed the fact that I had a job. So after a few conversations of trying to convince her to get me a rental and also giving her my word that I wouldn't have a gun in the car, she finally agreed so I could have a way to get back and forth to work in the winter.

After about two or three weeks of having the rental, one day Mark and I decided to get a bite to eat on our lunch break from the corner store up the block. There was a side street directly in front of our job where I would often park to eat lunch. So on this particular day as I was eating my lunch, I noticed a police car ride by super-slow, but I really didn't think too much of it. Minutes later, these same police officers were pulling up behind me with their red and blue lights on. Once again, I thought nothing of it and thought that I would be on my way after presenting the rental papers and my driving license. After the officer received my identification, he went back to his car and ran my name through the system. After what seemed to be a long wait, he finally came back to the jeep.

"What are you doing parked on this side street?" asked the officer.

"I work across the street at the Stocking Company. Is there a problem, Officer?" I asked.

"Yes, we have to tow this jeep because it's not in your name."

"Well, Officer, this rental belongs to a lady friend of mine, and she let me drive it so I could get back and forth to work during the winter. If you like, I could give her a call to verify that."

"There's no need, you can't be driving around a rental that's not in your name."

"No disrespect, Officer, I've driven and been pulled over in many rental cars, and I have never had a problem."

"Okay! Well, we do things different on this side of town. I'm going to give you a minute to get all your belongings out the jeep, and I need you to leave the keys inside."

"No problem, Officer!" I said. Not only did I leave the keys inside the jeep, I also locked the doors.

As I walked off I couldn't help but to think how this all seemed odd. Was it the Feds? I can't recall the exact amount I had spent on the rental, but it was at least $500, which was nonrefundable. Once again, I couldn't win for losing. Now it was the point where this job was costing me more money than I could afford to lose. Because of the embarrassment I felt for getting the rental taken at my job in front of everybody, I quit the next day.

The next day I woke up feeling like I had failed so many people around me who believed in my change and that I would have a successful transition. Overall I felt that I had failed myself. Even though in my mind I was stuck with the thought, I did the best I could. I must admit that change wasn't easy. I learned the hard way that it's the unexpected situations that will discourage you the most. For years I had spent my days leading by example in my neighborhood. I was known for keeping a sack and a pocket full of money. Now I was living a life where my pride was finally starting to eat at my conscious. I was barely getting by.

Outside of my immediate family, my queens were the most important people in my life. I felt like I owed them my all for holding me down while I was in the county. I spoke with Jenna about my struggles and my plans to start back hustling. Her initial reply was "I'm surprised you lasted that long." At this point in my relationship with Jenna, I believe she was over me, but at the same time she couldn't stand the thought of me being with any other female. I also spoke with Millini about my struggles and my plans to start back hustling. I could tell that she was upset, but she assured me that she understood. She also took the time to fill out job applications for me online. I'm sure at the end of the day, they both felt like it was only a matter of time. I went almost three months without selling drugs, which was the longest I had ever went. Minus the discouragement, I must say I was proud of myself for going that long.

It was time to put my next money move back in action. I knew a young hustler in my neighborhood who had that sack. He was one of the guys that had watched me come up grinding, and now he was making a name for himself hustling. So I reached out to him. I explained to him that I didn't want to step back into hustling full speed and that I would only be buying bubbles daily depending on how the day was going. I still had real fears about these unknown enemies I may have attracted from the boggish case. The next move was to go find a few of my loyal customers I had in the past, which wasn't hard. This also included me buying a second phone. The next move was to set up a trap station. I had a loyal customer that was like family: Sherly, a.k.a. Aunt-T. She had been there for me since my Twenty-Fifth and Parker days, through my ups and downs, raids, and the whole nine. Even though I didn't trust her, she always made sure to create a safe space where I could sit while waiting on the next phone call. I wouldn't let my clients come to her house, so that way I didn't have to worry about the traffic drawing police attention. The last move I made was put a "For Sale" sign on my SS. People who knew me knew I loved that car. So this was a very hard thing for me to do.

Everything was set in motion, and I was back answering calls, making enough money to make sure my bills were getting paid. I also added a new hustle to my plan. I had a female pit bull puppy (honey bunch bloodline) that my homegirl Latrice (rental car) had been holding down for me. She ended up falling in love with the dog. But once the dog became in heat, along with some other personal things, she decided it was time to give the dog back. I moved the dog to my trap station. The next day, I took her to breed with a relative by the name of Bling who had a stout stud from the Razor edge bloodline. They ended up having ten puppies, which meant $500 for a female pup and $350 for the males. This was free money. I was slowly sticking cash back into my safe. Regardless of my financial progress, mentally I was still living a paranoid life, riding around with a gun, and struggling with my fear of death.

One day I was riding around solo in my mustang making moves. I recall meeting up with Millini. I can't recall why, but she got to arguing with me. I believe in between that altercation she kicked my car and later handed me a duffle bag, which included nothing inside but my gym gear. But as soon as I pulled off from Millini, within the next few blocks I was getting pulled over by the police. I tucked my gun into the hidden compartment and proceeded to pull over. Once again, one thing I didn't do after the false arrest was smoke marijuana. Marijuana always seemed to make me more paranoid than I already was. Plus, I recognized it slowed down my reaction time. The last thing I needed was to be slowed or unfocused.

The Fear of Death

"Do we have a problem, Officer?" I asked.

"Yes," he replied, "you didn't use your signal on your turn coming out the parking lot. Can I see your license and registration?"

This was the first lie he told, because I always signaled. And this also confirmed that he had been watching me talk with Millini in the parking lot and must have seen her give me the bag and thought it was a drop-off.

"Here's everything you need," I said, handing him the requested paperwork.

After spending a few minutes at his car, another police car arrived on site. He and his support officer spoke for a brief moment, then came back to my car.

"Mr. Jones, is that marijuana I smell?"

"No, sir, I don't smoke marijuana."

"What's that on your lap? It looks like ashes to me."

"In my defense, sir, if you take a closer look you will see that it's ashes burning from my cigarette that's right there in the ash tray I just put out when you pulled me over."

"Looks like marijuana to me," he implied, "and that's probable cause to search your car." This would be the second lie the officer told. "Keep your hands where I can see them, and step out."

After about five minutes of searching the car and trunk, they found nothing. But I could tell he had a special interest in the bag Millini just gave me.

"Here's your paperwork. I saw you leave that parking lot talking to your girl. We are watching you, Clown. See you soon," said the officer before he got back into his car.

My first thought was "Did he just really call me by my street name?" I knew he meant business. My second thought was "I'm sure glad he didn't find my gun." My final thought was "Was this the Feds?" I left the scene more paranoid than I had been in a while. *Who do these people think I am?* I shut down shop for the next few weeks and only did business on the west side of town. I found myself once again isolating, bouncing from house to house, having sex multiple times a day, oversleeping, and turning to liquor as a way to suppress my boredom and cope. I was getting to the point where I had totally lost my ambition to hustle, mainly because I wasn't trying to go sit in nobody's prison. My circle of friends was already small, but I started to question the few I had. Can one of my guys be a rat? One aspect of my life I always pride myself on was I didn't let people get close to me; you had to be certified or a super-OG to be in my circle. But if I'm being honest, I felt that there was one loose end. This older cat from Hoovas by the name of Jean-Jaccet, who I pretty much learned how to perfect my hustle from, was for sure questionable due to some of our past experiences. Even though he has always been someone I respected, I made the decision to fall back on being around him so much.

As I was dealing with life the best way I know how, one day Millini came home and said, "I got a surprise for you outside." Confused, I grabbed my gun and went. I was so mentally disturbed at this time. I remember following her, looking at the back of her head, thinking to myself, *If she's trying to set me up, I will put a bullet right through it.* But that wasn't the case. When I exited the door, there it sat, a 2008 Dodge Charger on twenty-inch chrome rims. At this point I had been keeping it dope boy simple, riding old-schools and rentals. But I always had a passion for cars, and this car sure did reenergize me. I had been receiving many offers for my SS but had turned down all offers. After getting the Charger, I decided that I could finally let the SS go. I decided to put the car on the Internet and got the full cash offer I wanted in less than a week. After going on a neighborhood tour to show guys my new car, one stop I made was at Jean-Jaccet's house. For some reason, I remember thinking I wanted him to be proud of me. I would make the case that he and Nightmare were my two street role models, so of course I wanted to share this moment with him.

The day came to sell my SS, and I got every single dollar from the asking price. I waited a few days before I put my money move plan in motion. This time I knew things had to look different, and hustling would have to be my second priority. It seemed as if the universe knew what I was thinking. I got a call the next day from T-Stubb, an OG from Hoovas. He had the opportunity to coach a third-grade basketball team for the YMCA and wanted to know

The Fear of Death

if I would assist him in coaching. I jumped right on the opportunity with no questions asked. Being a coach fits somewhere in my top five proudest moments. I enjoyed every second of being around those kids and teaching them the basketball knowledge I had with the hopes of raising their basketball IQ. This was the moment in my life where I acknowledged within myself that there was a battle going on inside me that had been taking place since the birth of my son, Kingzton—La'Ron versus Clown. One of the sad realities of me being a coach was that I couldn't seem to shake this fear of death. On every single practice and game, I had my gun with me in my gym bag.

T-Stubb and Jean-Jaccet were close friends, so the more I found myself around T-Stubb, the more I was starting to be back around Jean-Jaccet. At this point in my life, I haven't been in a single shootout since I left the county jail in September 2013, so it's been about three or four months. One day T-Stubb and Jean-Jaccet invited me to go to the club, so I went. As I was sitting at the bar, sipping Hennessey, minding my business, this guy I knew to be from South Family Project approached me.

"What's up?" he said.

I guess he thought that I was going to be scared or cop out since I was basically solo, because neither Jaccet or Stubb gangbanged.

"You know what's up, RIP Maxxo!" I responded.

Maxxo was my friend who died at a club in South Omaha in 2009. We exchanged a few more words, and with no hesitation, I went straight to the car to grab my gun. Somehow Jean-Jaccet and T-Stubb both disappeared, but that's another story. I and the South Family guys spotted each other a few blocks away from the club, and without hesitation we both got to firing shots. Outside of some car damage, no harm was done. From that moment forward, I found myself back on offense, back on high alert, taking no chances. I guess in that moment I realized that just because I wanted to change, it didn't mean the world around me was changing, especially if I was still living in Omaha. Here I was just having a good time not looking for a problem, but a problem had a way of finding me. The advice I would give anybody who finds themselves in this position is to move out of town and give yourself a fair chance in another environment. For me, this was the moment where I should have left town and gave myself a better chance at succeeding.

Sometime had went by, and my life was at a standstill. On top of the three queens I already had, I added two new women to my life. This was creating a whole slew of problems with Jenna and Millini. I was back going to the club every other weekend with guys from Hoovas, throwing money and always buying overpriced champagne bottles. I was back smoking marijuana and paranoid as ever. I later got into two more shootouts since the club situation. Basketball season was over, so I was no longer coaching. I wrecked my charger and also had to buy three new pairs of rims in a matter of four months due to me cracking/curb checking them in the winter. The worse one of them all, I would have to say, was battling with post-traumatic street disorder and coping with liquor. Once again, when it came to drinking, I never saw myself as having an addiction, mainly because I could afford to pay for whatever I wanted to drink. My perception of an alcoholic was a bum or the old heads sitting in front of the liquor store waiting for you to come out with your spare change. But now that I look back, I would say there were three issues at the root of my life problems: being abandoned as a child, alcoholism, and overall an enormous amount of gun violence. Let me remind you, everything up to this point happened when I was twenty-three or younger. So as scientist would say, my brain wasn't even fully developed.

At this time I would say I had three good things going for me: one, I was alive; two, I was still present as much as possible in Kingzton's life; three, in some ways I was still portraying to be broke because my queens were paying a few of my bills and I didn't want that to stop, but I was still loading up my safe. I went from a few hundred dollars after losing my job. Fast-forward to four months later I was up $8,000 with assets. Once again, my love for cars put me in the position where I was hustling backward. I had been having my eyes on this 1987 Chevy Brougham. I had finally gotten the call that he was ready to sell it without the rims. So I immediately jumped on it. I ended up paying $2,500 for the car, $1,500 on some 22' Joe Martin rims. I put it in the paint shop with the plans to get it painted Houston Astros blue with an orange top, with the Astros symbol on the doors. As a side note, I went to prison before I was able to finish the car, but I've had plenty of dreams, really nightmares, of me getting shot up in that exact car. I know people would have been able to easily identify me in that car, and those dreams could have easily been my reality.

On March 5, 2014, Milton and I got together to catch up. I counted up a little over $5,000 and made plans to visit the "Hood Nick Car Show" event that took place in our hometown, Dumas, Arkansas, every year around the end of March. My hope was to bump into one of my childhood friends and find a new connect. My mom's birthday is March 7, so I figured I would splurge with her for her birthday, then grind hard for the next few weeks before I headed out. On March 6, I woke up like any other day. I made love to Jenna, took a shower, ironed my clothes and got dressed, ate breakfast, fed my dog, grabbed my gun, and out the door I went to the local gas station to put $25 in the tank. I bought a pint of vodka and a pack of Newport long cigarettes, and I was ready for the day.

I had been riding around making money moves when I got a call from Milton asking if I wanted to ride with him. I parked my car and put my gun up because Milton didn't have license, and he was in a rental. We drove around till about eleven in the evening before going to the liquor store and getting my mom some liquor for her birthday. I bought her a bottle of Moet Rose and a fifth of raspberry Ciroc. We stayed at her house partying until a little past twelve. Then I dropped my sister Pra'Shae off at her house and got back in traffic moving around the city. Shortly after, I met up with Jenna who had just left a Miley Cyrus concert and had been blowing my phone up ridiculously before I got to her. After chatting with her I told Milton to take me back to my car, which he did. Before we decided to split, Milton asked me to follow him, which I did. I didn't ask any questions nor thought nothing of it because this was something we had done multiple times in the past as a way to stunt. But what I was about to get myself into was 100-percent unexpected.

REVIEW BOOK CLUB QUESTIONS.

La'Ron "Clown" Jones Post Traumatic Street Disorder Vol. 1

CHAPTER 10

State of Nebraska versus Jones

We pulled up to a house that was familiar to me. I had known this to be a house that belonged to an associate of Milton's baby mama's house. As I pulled up I thought to myself, *Okay, it's time to party,* because I could tell from the scene that some type of gathering was taking place. Milton pulled up, and I pulled up directly behind him. He got out his car super-fast without giving me any notice on what we were doing there. It was this moment that I was a little taken back by Milton's actions, his movements.

As I sit here and write this, I ponder on the thought, what if Milton's negative feelings came about when I went to visit Jenna at the concert and he saw how we were interacting, how Jenna didn't want to leave my side that night? Maybe that made him get in his head in a way that he wanted to confront his baby mama about whatever their issue was, which until this day I still don't have an answer nor understand why Milton flipped so quick when he was just cool as can be.

I watched from a distance, looking at Milton and her argue. Within a matter of seconds their arguing turned to a physical altercation. Of course my initial thought was that he was tripping, but at the same time, I personally felt that what they had going on was none of my business. I can't recall who but I remember one of her friends yelling, "Get your homeboy!" to which I replied, "That's on them, that ain't got nothing to do with me." But I guess since I didn't respond to her cry for help, two other guys who were already at the party decided they would, and that's when it became my problem. As soon as I observed these two guys force their way between Milton and engage to jump him, I immediately jumped in to defend Milton. Milton weighed less than I did, so I rushed the biggest of the two guys, asking no questions. To be honest, I was semi-drunk from my mom's birthday party, and this tussle took me a little longer than I expected. But after I finally got the guy to the ground and stumped him out, I told Milton, "Let's go, you're tripping." I was more than sure Milton was feeling the Moet and Ciroc as well. As we began to leave, extra words were being exchanged by Milton and his baby mama, and that's when I noticed a guy walking from the porch, leaving his place of safety, clutching his waist as if he had a gun. Without hesitation, I pulled out my gun and fired two warning shots in the air. Then I immediately pointed at him and started firing. I later found out that he was struck twice; once in the leg and the fatal shot hit him in the neck. With all respect to my victim, I never saw him pull out a gun, so this is not me making an excuse for what I did as self-defense. But from the street life I lived and experienced, a post-traumatic street mentality was formed, which created a mindset that operated off survival—killed or be killed—so even faking like you had a gun contributed to triggering my post traumatic street disorder.

True story: the moment I upped my gun, it seemed as if a satanic figure was sitting on my shoulder. There were no words mentioned; it was just present, observing my actions. The next morning as I lay in my bed thinking about all that had taken place, I couldn't seem to get this satanic figure out my head. What did this mean? What did it represent? It brought me back to the time I was shot and I felt the power of God lift me off the ground. If I had experienced the power of God, then seeing this satanic figure was equally valid. Furthermore, the thought of the battle between La'Ron versus Clown was also at the forefront of my thoughts. While doing so, I found myself doing something that I had never done before: questioning my actions.

Even though harming another person is never the answer, there was a long period of time in life that I didn't regret anything that I had done in my past. But this time was different.

I remember growing up watching my grandma and my mom being abused by men, seeing scars, hearing them cry, me feeling helpless, and them having those conversations with me on how a man should never put his hands on a woman. So early on in my life, I developed a deeply rooted belief that a man should never hit a woman. Furthermore, I'm my mom's oldest child and resided in a house with all females, which included my three younger sisters that I had always been overly protective over. Once again, I grew up in a house with five uncles and I was the youngest. I believe their examples of protecting each other poured into Milton and I's friendship. Since the first day I met Milton, he was like the little brother I never had. There was not one time I allowed anyone to harm him in any type of way. I made a promise to him when we were kids after I beat up his bully in the projects, and more than ten years later, I was still standing firm on that promise.

On the flip side, I grew up as a teenager searching for a place to fit in this new state of Omaha, Nebraska, searching for acceptance and respect. I soon found out that the values were different from family life and street life. These street values came with a message of "death before dishonor." In that moment when Milton was fighting his baby mama, I lost sight of the great values that I had learned as a kid, respecting women, etc., which resulted to killing a man behind an altercation that I knew was morally wrong.

Before I end with Milton, might I add there was a time when Milton did a small prison bid, and I was one phone call away his whole number. On many occasions, I gave his other baby mama money to put on his books and even sent pictures. On two different occasions, I took both of our sons to the mall and bought them matching shoes. When Milton was released, I was at the front door to pick him up, like a scene out a movie, with a cell phone that already had a few clients calling, some money, and a sack—all at no cost. Since my incarceration, I've heard from Milton one or two times. He wrote me a letter, which I still have, but in that letter he assured me that "We all we got. I got you. Whatever you need, let me know." I can't recall my exact reply, but I remember telling him, "Just check on me from time to time, and I don't need money but pick my son up every now and then take him out to eat and tell him it's from his dad." I or my son haven't heard from Milton since.

So less than forty-eight hours after the shooting, I woke up to a loud knock at the door and my dog Tyson going crazy. "Police Department, open the door!" I did and I was met by a shield and numerous guns pointed in my direction. "Put your hands up and don't move. You have an arrest warrant for first-degree murder."

The moment leading up to my arrest, I was in denial that it was me the police was looking for. I, for sure, thought they were after Milton. As I was riding in the police car, I knew that it could possibly be the last moment that I would live my life as a free man. Six months after being released for a murder I didn't commit, I was headed back to Douglas County Jail on a new case. I went through the booking process which seemed like forever, and afterward I was moved to a maximum security unit. Of course coming through the doors, I knew there would be a real possibility that I had to fight, but I've had county time before and had never been in a fight, mainly because I always seemed to know and be cool with those who were most respected amongst their neighborhoods. But this time was different, and I believe officers who booked me in knew exactly where they were taking me.

As I entered the unit I saw a familiar face. This guy's name was Avery Tyler Sr., who was a rising star in the Nebraska basketball community but ended up catching a murder case. We had similar cases. I knew Avery because he had been in the county fighting his case when I left six months ago. Even though we were from rival hoods, I felt a little at ease seeing his face, but I still remained on point. I went to my assigned cell, which was upstairs, to drop my bag off, and as I took a seat on my bed I noticed a guy approaching my cell door. After taking a quick glance at him, mainly noticing his shoes tied tight and his shirt tucked, I knew what time it was. As he entered the entryway to my door, he looked back, as if he was checking to

State of Nebraska versus Jones

see where the guard was, or maybe his homie that later attempted to jump in the fight but was a few seconds too late. As soon as he took a look back, before he could turn his head and look back my way, I hit him with a right hook, which I knew stung him. I grabbed his collar with my left hand and swung many times as I could with my right hand, bagging him up with every punch I threw. Out the side of my eye, I spotted another guy approaching me at a high rate of speed, so I let his homie go and ran down the stairs toward this mop I had seen on my way in. I had plans to Bruce Lee them both, but before I had the chance, the guards ran in.

I went to the hole for a week, mostly where I dealt with my thoughts, reflecting on my life and trying to sleep the days away. After a day or so, I finally got the info on the dude that I had fought. And it had nothing to do with what I was arrested for. He had beefed with me behind the murder I had been acquitted for. On my second day in the hole, I got a knock at my door. "You are about to be on the news!" A top official was being interviewed about my case. To my surprise, he made a statement that I was guilty before any discovery was ever shown, saying, "We got him now. He's not getting away this time." I remember thinking to myself how unjust his statement was. This was another sign that there was no way they planned on playing fair, in respect to my due process. I can't say I didn't understand this county official's frustration because by this point, my name had been brought up in murders. I had been interrogated for several murders I was accused of committing. My name had been on several warrants to raid trap houses. I had been caught with or near several guns. I've had several cases dismissed. There was an untrue rumor that I was the shot caller for the Hoova Crips and had a hit man. Even the fact that I was constantly getting shot and surviving may have been frustrating for some as well. If you were to look at my actual arrest history, one could easily assume my only problem was driving without license. Regardless of my past, I had never been convicted to prison time due to so many of my cases being dismissed.

Shortly after my arrest, my attorneys came to see me, which were the same two attorneys I had from my previous cases. We didn't discuss much aside from them wanting to know if I was innocent or guilty so they could prepare for what to look forward to, I suppose. Of course I told them that I was innocent and even brought up my past, the comment the top official made on the news, with the hopes for them to believe the system was against me because they had been trying to convict me but failed and that this was another attempt. They stated that we would discuss the case more after we got the discovery.

    Months had went by before I finally received my discovery. My attorneys sent a private investigator to the county jail to go over my discovery with me. This was strange mostly because this guy just sat in the room and watched me the whole time and offered no type of legal advice. It was unusual, but I was just happy to finally be able to look at who the witnesses were and their statements. This was for sure a stressful process, but I was invested, taking my time and as many notes as I could. As I was going through my paperwork, I discovered that Jenna made a statement. Immediately after the shooting took place, I called Jenna to come pick me up. So in that way, she was involved but never charged with any crimes. Her statement said that she picked me up, but didn't see me with a gun that night. She went on to tell the police what I was wearing that night and directed them to where the clothes were in our apartment. Initially I was upset because she had been continually putting money on my books and coming to visit me, and she never mentioned that she was questioned nor that she gave statements to the detectives. But after dissecting her statements and comparing it to other statements, I realized that what she said was more helpful than harmful, because it showed flaws in the witnesses' statements on what they said I was wearing. This opened the door for me to ask the court to test the clothing I was wearing that night for gun residue, because I knew they would come back clean, but for some strange reason they denied it and said if I wanted to get them tested I could pay for them myself. I'm sure they knew that was impossible since they confiscated my money during my arrest and said I couldn't get it back till trial was over. I also discovered that there were four people who said they saw me shoot the gun, but all four people gave different descriptions of what clothing I had on. After the detectives collected all these inconsistent statements, they created a six-man lineup, placing my photo in the lineup twice, in box 5 and box 6. Even worse, during this process they had doors open while they were doing interviews. One guy even had a cellphone and made a call.

So as I was learning all this new information and remaining innocent, I was thinking there is no way they will ever be able to get pass the fact that my right to due process had been violated multiple times. As I was discovering all these flaws in my case, two things were clear: one, that the state had no intentions on playing fair; two, if I couldn't win on a motion, I was going to trial. Damn if I do and damn if I don't! On top of all that, my victim was Caucasian.

Before I proceed, let me take a minute to discuss what I see as a problem for me and so many others who find themselves battling against the law when you're poor, on top of being Black and being gang-affiliated. The case for many of us is, we damn if we do and damn if we don't. So why not fight? Our life experience doesn't seem to matter, only what we are being charged for. With the proper evaluations, the record would reflect that most gang members have PTSD. With utmost respect, why do we only reserve this as a defense for first responders, police officers, medics, firefighters, vets, etc.? Sad to say, I've been in so many gun battles I lost count. I've witnessed so much death that you would think my life was a movie. One thing is for sure, my experiences have created a mentality for me that's not normal. Furthermore, not once was I asked about my experiences, my background, my mentality when I was in the county jail preparing to fight my case. And for those who do get asked, there's a fear that they will use what we said against us in court. Another issue that's never spoken about is the lack of oversight we have in this state when it comes to those who are prosecuting these cases. They continue to throw young gang members' lives away without taking into consideration that people do change. I was sentenced to life plus forty years. Where is the hope, the redemption, the justice in a sentence such as that? History has shown us that prosecutors are the most influential voices in the criminal justice system. They have almost unlimited power to push for the maximum punishment, often in ways that are largely hidden from taxpayers' and defendants' view. Their systematic focus on obtaining convictions and securing severe prison sentences, instead of addressing the root cause of crime, is a major driver of mass incarceration that compounds racial disparities throughout the justice system.

Okay, enough on the personal. Let's get back to the purpose!

Once trial began, I sat there most of the time lost with the thought that these witnesses had been perfectly coached and has an answer for everything that my attorneys were asking. It was as if they had a transcript on what the questions would be. Regardless of the witnesses admitting to making contradicted statements, admitting to being drunk and/or on cocaine, all of their testimonies were allowed in court. Once the time came for Jenna to get on the stand, her testimony would once again open up another door for me to fight. She testified that she was shown a photo lineup of another unidentified male and had identified a person that was with me after picking me up after the shooting. This information/photo lineup was not a part of my discovery, nor disclosed to my attorneys. When my attorney questioned the detectives on the whereabouts of this photo lineup in which Jenna made a positive identification, the detective stated confidently, "I threw that photo lineup in the trash."

And from what I knew about the law, this was a major Brady Violation, but of course it was overruled and we continued. This only supported my theory that from the jump I was never going to have a fair trial because as one of the top officials said, "We got him this time. He's not getting away." My prosecutor even wore a neck tie during trial that read, "Winning isn't everything. It's the only thing." After five days of trial and a few hours of deliberation, I was found guilty for first-degree murder. I wasn't mad. I didn't cry. I just thought about Kingzton and how he would grow up being another fatherless child.

Before my sentencing date, I had a meeting with a clergy named Chaplin Ron, to whom my cellmate Q-11 connected me with. I knew of Chaplin Ron from my DCYC days but had never developed any type of bond with him. As I was talking to him about my state of mind at the time, I expressed that I wanted to speak to my victim's family even after being advised that it wasn't a good idea. His advice was "A captain is always in control of his ship. If the ship was to sink, the captain should always remain behind the wheel. And in doing so, the final decision/word will be his." We went on to pray that God watch over me, and shortly after I watched him as he disappeared behind a secure door. This was when I told myself that I was going to go to prison and change my life. I haven't seen Chaplin Ron since then.

My sentencing date was April 1, 2015. Yeah, April Fool's Day. All my charges were read, and as I mentioned before, I was given a life sentence plus forty years. Before the sentence was given, I was asked if I had anything to say. I replied, "Yes, Your Honor."

"All right. Mr. Jones, this is probably your last time to speak, if there's anything you would like to say, sir. Would you like to say anything?" was the judge's exact words.

As I stood up to speak, I glanced at my lawyer, who looked up at me as if she was thinking, "What are you doing? Sit down." I thought to myself, *I'm the captain of this ship, and I can't go down without speaking.*

"Yes, Your Honor. I would like to say that I'm not admitting guilt, but I and my family's blessing goes out to Mr. Samuel's family. I understand what happened was not right. I woke up today, I prayed, I asked God to take this situation and make me better and not bitter. I ask y'all to do the same. I came into this courtroom and saw my prosecutor wearing a tie. It said, 'Winning isn't everything. It's the only thing.' There are people in this system that don't care about justice. They just care about convictions. I know you all have. There were plenty of you all in this court, and you all heard the case. And at the end of day, I just ask that you all just pray. Just like I said, if you believe, just pray for me, and I'll pray for myself to not let this situation make me bitter, but make me better. Thank you, everybody, for listening."

It wasn't a written speech, but it was from the heart. After giving my speech to the court, I remember looking at my mom and noticing that she was sitting there stuck, in shock, not moving at all as the judge sentenced me to *death by incarceration.*

Once I got to the Diagnostic and Evaluation Center (D&E), which is where you go to get evaluated before you are transferred to prison, I realized that the people I thought would be in my corner for emotional support had a stopping point; out of sight, out of mind, as they say. Everyone who was in my corner was slowly drifting off. Growing up, I would always hear stories about how people would leave their loved ones behind once they went to prison. Of course, I was one of those guys who thought this would never happen to me because I had a small circle and built a tight crew. I had been in the streets for years condoning in illegal activities and never had a friend rat on me. I had been in and out the county jail, cheated on my three queens, and one way or another I could always go back to them. Deep down inside I felt like all the relationships I built in the streets had been put to the test, and they had passed with flying colors. Even though Jenna had gotten on the stand against me and could have possibly hurt me if she knew more, I was willing to forgive her and allow her to come see me. I had been with her since a teen, so mentally it was hard to lose her. But while I was in D&E, I didn't get one visit. During my years of hustling, I had showed a lot of financial love to those around me, and it was hard seeing that love not being reciprocated at the lowest point of my life.

But guess who did come see me? The Feds! I was told that I had a legal visit and I thought it was my attorneys, so I got dressed and went. When I got to a room near intake, I saw two unfamiliar faces and later spotted an FBI badge. I was curious as to what they had to say, because one thing for sure, I knew it had nothing to do with the murder. Obviously, they were there for a different reason.

"Hello, Mr. Jones. How are you doing?" the lady agent asked.

"The best I can be," I replied.

"Are you willing to speak with us?" asked the agent.

"Sure. What is this about?" Instantly one of the agents pulled out a small recording device.

"Well, it's about prostitution," the agent said as she opened a folder revealing my photo on top of a stack of papers about God knows what.

"Pimping? I don't know what you are talking about, but I'm ready to leave this room right now. If you have any further questions, please contact my lawyers."

This only confirmed my belief that the Feds had been watching me. I spent nine months in D&E before I was transferred to the Nebraska State Penitentiary.

On my first day at the penitentiary, I must admit that I was nervous. Not scared nervous, more of just an unfamiliar nervous of being in a new environment. Plus, I had been gangbanging in the streets for years, so I knew I would have to answer for some of the things that I had done. As I was leaving turnkey (booking/holding), the first thing I spotted was a blind man and a dog, and the crazy part about this was they weren't even together. So now I was really tripping, thinking, *What in the world!* Within minutes I noticed a few guys, who I figured were all from Hoovas, waiting on me, and I was right. I later got introduced to a couple more guys from Hoovas who were all old heads. I recognized one familiar face, a guy named Boston from my 1967 Plymouth days, because I used his house a few months to stash my car/drugs. Also, there was a guy there who I had always grown up hearing stories about and even compared myself to as a way to connect my street success with neighborhood history. Yes, this would be the same guy I mentioned in chapter 6, Bernard "Nardo" Long. Shortly after meeting with the Hoova guys, I went back to my unit and, to no surprise, I had guys lined up waiting for me, ready to interrogate me. On my first day there, I had five different guys from three different neighborhoods approach me about murders that I had supposedly committed, and my answer was the same for all of them: "I don't know anything about that!" But at the same time, my posture was firm. Luckily, I didn't get into any fights, which contributed to all these guys I was questioned about whether I killed them or not were from other Crip neighborhoods. And luckily, at the time I came through the prison door, the focus was on trying to get all the Crip hoods to unite. After having a conversation with the guy that was leading the Crip card, he spoke about how he had heard about me and knew I was solid. He assured me that I was cool and wouldn't have any problems unless it was organized to be a one-on-one fight. This opened the door for me to do my time in a way that I could focus less on street problems and more on being a voice for Hoovas when it came to prison politics.

Even though there was a shot caller for the Crip Card who would converse/mediate with other hoods and races, there was also a shot caller for every hood. Within a matter of six months, I was given *the keys* as the shot caller for all the Hoova Crips. Being given this power would be another factor that steered me toward my personal change. My message as a leader was about self-respect, unity, money, staying on top of your hygiene/keeping your clothes ironed, and most importantly getting your GED or high school diploma. At this time I was against programs/programming. On the flip side of this story, I found myself up against the powerful drug K2. As a leader, it was a major challenge to keep guys organized when they were impaired all day long. I didn't use it, but many guys around me did, and based on what I was witnessing, these guys would get high and was a poor excuse for what it meant to be a man or set a examples for the younger guys that were coming through the prison doors. One way or another, I kept finding myself at odds with guys around me about the past and present. This put me in a position where I had to seriously evaluate the guys I had around me and myself and what I stood for as a man behind these prison walls.

As I was dealing with the daily prison politics and watching guys I cared about, certified gangsters, street ballers, and so many others turn into zombies/K2 addict in a matter of months, I was also dealing with my own personal problems and money issues. I got a few dollars on my books on top of my cigarette hustle, but I needed more cash to buy a TV, shoes, etc. I had $1,000 cash I left with one of my immediate family members to hold till I got to prison. Once I called and told her I needed the money, she said she had to spend it on bills. I had the money that was confiscated from me when I got arrested, which the court wouldn't release until after my direct appeal had been finalized. I had invested $4,050, which after going to prison I never received one red cent back, so that was a loss. I had just purchased the Chevy Brougham for $2,500, plus another $1,500 for the rims, which I gifted my mom for her birthday in 2015, so I didn't get money back off what I invested into the car. And to add to all these, I soon got a letter in the mail saying that I lost my direct appeal.

As I was dealing with all these unexpected situations and adapting to prison life, I found myself reflecting on a lot of the same feelings I had as a motherless and fatherless child—feelings of abandonment. I left the streets as a twenty-three-year-old young man touching five figures on a regular. Now more than a year later, I'm in prison with basically nothing but the respect I earned from the street life—no money, no family visit, no consistent financial support. I was not seeing my son; it was just me and the life sentence. I found myself working in the prison kitchen for over six months for .76¢ a day. Child support took everything except $10 a month. But the goal was to work this job till I was able to get a job at "The Shop" where I could get paid $1.08 an hour so I could support myself while incarcerated. Even worse, I was locked down in a twelve-by-six box every night replaying old memories and being confronted by my demons. I had sleepless nights, and I woke up in cold sweats. Every time it was locked down and the doors slammed shut or popped open, I would have light panic attacks and flashbacks of shootouts. I had no one I felt I could trust or talk to about what I was dealing with, so I went to see a mental health doctor and of course they had no answer aside from putting me on medication. I took myself off the medicine after about three months of feeling worse than I had before.

There's a quote that reads, "If you live for the world's acceptance, you will die from its rejection." And that's where I was at mentally, slowly dying inside. Shortly after I entered the prison system, once again, it was as if a domino effect had occurred, and I was now watching guys from Hoovas, mostly younger beings sentenced to life in prison. Akeem was convicted for first-degree murder and two cases of accessory to murder. Burger was convicted for two first-degree murders. HB was convicted for two first-degree murders and two attempts. Stay Ready was convicted for first-degree murder. Mook was convicted for first-degree murders, and Cin-Locc, a close friend, was convicted for first-degree assault and was sentenced to a de facto life sentence. The truth remains that, one way or another, we all had an impact on each other's lives in more negative ways than positive. As I begin to see so many of my guys go through the same emotions and similar situations as I did—managing doing time, not talking to

Bernard or older lifers, watching so-called OGs give out hypocritical advice, etc.—I felt that I could be the support in their life that Bernard had been to me and I could lead by example and show them what it meant to "do the time and not let the time do you." I knew I had a slight advantage because one thing I didn't lose was my street respect, and the question I kept asking myself at this time was, am I going to keep misleading these young guys who are looking up to me, or am I'm going to show them that it's okay to step away from the gang life in order to be your best self? And Bernard "Nardo" Long helped me discover the answer to this question.

While I was dying inside, Bernard walked up to me every day and asked me a series of the same questions.

"How are you doing today, lil bro?" Bernard would ask.

"I'm good," I would reply most times as I kept walking.

"How's your son doing?" he would always ask if I stopped to talk.

"He's good, growing up fast," I would often reply, too embarrassed to say I haven't talk to Kingzton.

"Having a life sentence is hard, right? Trust me, I know." Bernard would always find a way to ask me about doing time.

"I'm coo'!" I would often reply, hiding the pain I was feeling.

"You should sign up for some self-betterment clubs and programs," Bernard would always suggest.

"I got too much time. What will a program do for me? It's a waste of time," I would always say.

Even though Bernard had always been someone I looked up to from a gang-life perspective, a lot had changed about him; he was not the same person I had heard about growing up. For that very reason, I went a long period of time without talking to Bernard. But he was consistent, and there wasn't a day that he didn't ask how I was doing. One day Bernard came to me and said, "They are about to start a new year-long program, the Prison Fellowship Academy. You should sign up. Only forty people will be allowed to participate, and you might be able to get in since you don't get write-ups, so put in an inmate request form."

"Okay, I'll think about it," I replied, finally giving him a different answer.

And of course we continued to have these conversations before I finally signed up for the academy and made the cut. At this point, I had taken a few classes while incarcerated, but this was the first program I signed up for. This was the beginning of my journey from boyhood to manhood.

REVIEW BOOK CLUB QUESTIONS.

PART 3

From Boyhood to Manhood

CHAPTER 11

The Importance of Educating Yourself while Incarcerated

I ended part 1 of this book on hypocritical advice and forgiving others. I ended part 2 of this book on the mentality created by living the gang life and the way that mentality distorts our ability to think clearly and regulate our emotions. I'm ending part 3 of this book on receiving advice, self-reflection, and most importantly, forgiving yourself.

* * * * *

I am one of those individuals that people said would never change. "La'Ron's a menace to society." In turn, to understand what I have been through and to see where I'm at today, this book is a testament to how much I had to overcome mentally. Ultimately, I understand the street experience that I went through is not just my experience, and this journey I've been on from certified gang member, to ex–gang member, to being a voice and example behind these prison walls for all those who seek to leave the gang life in the past sure doesn't have to be just my experience as well. And I'm hon-

The Importance of Educating Yourself while Incarcerated

ored to have been at the forefront of this mission when it comes to my generation inspiring the next generation. It has been that very thought that has kept me motivated to educate myself so I would always be prepared to pour into others. I don't proclaim to be perfect, nor do I have all the answers, but what I do know is that I have no desire, none whatsoever, to go back to the lifestyle of being a gangster. But adopting this mindset didn't happen overnight; it was surely a process.

So let's rewind. At the age of twenty-three, I was charged and later convicted for first-degree murder. I had dropped out of school my tenth-grade year, and a high percentage of my knowledge was based off survival instincts and street smarts. As a growing young man, there wasn't much that I knew about my self-worth. For me, self-worth was all about my image, being accepted, being respected, how others viewed/thought of me, masking my emotions, dressing in nice clothes, driving nice cars, selling drugs, womanizing, and overall, protecting the image of the character "Clown" I had created by doing what I had to do in the streets in order to be defined as a *real n*gga*. But, as I mentioned, somewhere in my life journey came this battle between La'Ron and Clown. As I began to take on the task of educating myself, I earned my high school diploma and also participated in other programs/classes that had an impact on my life; to name a few, Prison Fellowship Academy, Community Justice Center Victim Impact Class, 7 Habits of Highly Effective People, Intentional Peer Support, and Defy Ventures.

New exposure: As I mentioned before, my journey with Bernard was a rocky one. With the fact that he was one of the most certified gangsters from his generation, I couldn't wrap my mind around what had caused him to change, what had caused him to step away from the street fame that I'm sure took him years to earn. Like most youths who look at those who have stepped away from the gang, I found myself questioning his gangster. I found myself being very judgmental toward Bernard because not only did I feel like he was misrepresenting himself, but also the Hoova family and everything that we stood for. But as time went on, the advice I received from Bernard always seemed to come at a perfect time, and educating myself was always at the forefront of those conversations. But along with his advice came with me being watchful. Who was the man behind these messages/advice? As time went on, I was no longer seeing Bernard as a gangster, an OG, or this person that prison adversity had created. I started to see him as a mentor, a friend, a big brother.

The biggest barrier to wisdom is being judgmental.

I began to join the Lifer's Club meetings, putting myself around the guys that I would refer to as the wise men. The more I watched and listened, the more I was able to learn more about my own self-worth. They often spoke about their transgressions and what it took for them to overcome their old mentality. I learned from lifers such as Willie Tucker, Mike Sims, Todd Cook, Ron O'Neill, Lamont Arnold, Brian Perkins, Mike Anderson, Wolfgang, Robert Nave, Earnest Jackson, Rodney Mason, and Avery Tyler Sr. This offered me the insight on how to do my time and not let the time do me.

Even though a major shift had begun to take place in my life, I still had one piece of that post-traumatic street disorder mentality holding me back, which was judging others off street standards and principles, mainly because even in prison I still had the mindset that I would only associate with real n*ggas, and I would avoid snitches, lames, and those who have crimes that are frowned upon. But this all changed once I was approved to participate in the Prison Fellowship Academy (PFA). This is a Christian-based program that operates on six core values: productivity, responsibility, restoration, affirmation, and the two core values that had a major impact on my life, community and integrity.

Community. The program was set up for all those who were approved (forty individuals). They had to live in the same housing unit and gallery. What this did was put me around the very people that I told myself I would stay away from. Being a part of this new PFA community environment created a shift in how I started to view other individuals. As I began to identify the good in others, I had to do some major self-reflection. A part of this self-reflection came with me searching for forgiveness for things that I've done in my past. Then the question became, how could I continue to be a hypocrite, judging others, when I'm on my knees daily asking God for forgiveness? When I no longer began to judge people off their past and began to meet them where they were in life, I was able to get rid of that post-traumatic street disorder mentality of judging others off street standards, principles, and now values. I realized that good people are good people, and people make mistakes. I am no one's god, judge, or jury, so who am I to judge? Once I was able to forgive others, it taught me how to forgive myself. We are all imperfect humans!

Integrity. Integrity was a word that I didn't understand the meaning of until I was twenty-four years young. Sad but true. I often speak about words of value that has been misplaced when it comes to the gang culture, and the word *integrity* is for sure one. For example, real man versus real n*gga, family versus homies, community versus hood, and integrity versus death before dishonor. And for me that's exactly how I viewed integrity: death before dishonor. Being a part of a gang, you are taught to believe in having your guys back whether they were right or wrong. This way, having integrity doesn't exist. There would be times that I knew I was wrong, but for the sake of being there for my guys and having their back, I often went against what was morally right. Look at my case as an example. What the word *integrity* did for my life was major. It opened up the door for me to stop playing *both sides.* Even though I was stepping into my manhood, I would still give Crip handshakes to the Crips, I would still say "On my hood." In turn, the word *integrity* allowed me to create uncomfortable conversations on why I had decided to leave the gang life behind and how I would no longer be involved in any gang activity. Essentially, I realized if I needed to put my life on the line, continue to lose, or be taken away from my loved one's behind people who called themselves my friends, then I had the wrong kind of friends.

As I began on my journey of learning more about my self-worth and educating myself while incarcerated, I began to feel this new sense of hope. People do change! I also learned that there are a lot of guys in prison who want to change their life, but for numerous of reasons they struggle to do so. I would learn this through numerous of incarcerated individuals who were familiar with my street resumé, who would ask me, "How did you do it, La'Ron? You really did change!"

Guys would often ask me to schedule time to talk with them one-on-one, ask me to speak with some of their younger homies/family members, and the one that made me the proudest in that moment was the list of guys I had asking me to vouch for them to be a part of the PFA. Now after my participation, there were more gang members willing to participate and commit to joining this year-long program. How amazing is that? God had allowed me to be a light in such a dark place for the very people that our society tends to give up on. Due to a few bumps in the road, the first cohort graduated in eighteen months, which was an extra six months that we didn't sign up for. Afterward, I was asked to be a mentor for the PFA, which I continued to do so throughout my time at NSP.

For me, as things began to slow down in the PFA program, I began to hear about this new program that was catching my interest. I got wind of a program being offered to a select few, Intentional Peer Support. Similar to the PFA, you needed to be misconduct-free for an ample period of time, approved by the administration, and someone has to put in a word for you. Of course I checked all the boxes. Now all I had to do was play the waiting game. The IPS program operated off four tasks and three principles. The four tasks were connection, worldview, mutuality, and moving toward. The three principles were "From Helping to Learning Together," "Individual to Relationship," and "From Fear to Hope and Possibility." The goal is to build mutually responsible relationships in which you learn and grow with those who participate. But what made this program so special for those who graduated was you would now be allowed to set up an hour visit with incarcerated individuals in restrictive housing/the hole. I made the cut!

As of now, during my years of incarceration I have never been placed in restrictive housing. But, doing time, I would always hear these stories about guys who would go to the hole and lose their mind, so I understood for the guys in the hole to be allowed to talk with a peer while on 23 and 1 lockdown was a big deal for them as well. Similar to my journey in PFA, this also showed me how so many guys had it in their mind that they wanted to change their life for the better, but due to gang affiliation, addictions, financial problems (hustlers), or even mental health, they struggled to make that change. But on the flip side, I also would hear stories about guys who went to the hole and picked up a book that helped them be better individuals once they were released from the hole. After many visits to the hole and seeing how it impacted guys' mental health, I began to tell myself, "Any light you can get in a dark place is surely better than darkness."

One day, after taking a look at the book cart I noticed they had a slim collection of books, and even most of the books they did have had pages missing. Due to staff shortage, which were the people in charge of passing out books, there were several individuals whose needs weren't being met when it came to spiritual and other reading materials. I sought a wise man, Willie Tucker, who taught me how to write a proposal. With the knowledge gained, I began to draft a proposal to the Warden, respectfully requesting the approval to provide spiritual materials, devotionals, daily breads, brochures, newspapers, and a variety of different genre of books to the men in the hole. Shortly after submitting my proposal, the Warden approved it. And not only did she approve me to stock the book carts, I was also allowed to go door-to-door and pass out books. Thanks to PFA, NSP Library, and incarcerated individuals, on the first month alone 152 books were donated to restrictive housing book cart.

Also, while on my journey to visit many men in the hole, not only was I there to share my story of transformation and hope. I was also there building relationships and listening to their stories, their worldview on life, and the mindset that led them to prison or the hole. This often had both of us vulnerable and transparent about our lived experience. During these meetings I have seen so many hardcore gangsters cry; I've lost count. I would often think to myself, what if we, ex-gang members and active gang members, had a space to share these stories—our past experiences and how we overcame our transgressions—to these young guys that were entering the prison system? This thought would create the start of my next proposal.

As I began to ask myself a backward question, "What's the problem to this answer I had?" I began to study the state of the NSP prison culture. I began to realize that there was a generational gap that existed. Respectfully, the space we had where we could go to share these experiences was too small and also occupied by other clubs that had other goals. I knew in order for my idea to work I had to create a self-betterment club with bylaws to govern it. Even though I had a plan, I knew there was no way I could do it alone.

I knew my next move was to create an executive board, but first I had to find a vice president. I knew just the person for the mission: Avery Tyler Sr. Avery was once gang-affiliated but now was the pastor of the prison church. But there was one problem: similar to the mindset I once had, Avery didn't look at programming in a positive light. In the summer of 2020, after an hour-long conversation we had on the yard, looking around at our environment, we found ourselves feeling disheartened, sympathizing and empathizing the effects that prison have had on all of our lives ranging from substance abuse, depression, lack of family support, and for most the division that are perpetually created by the gang life. Afterward, Avery assured me that he was all-in. Avery and I began meeting to lay the groundwork to propose something radical that had never been done before in any Nebraska prison. We had moved away from the idea of creating the typical club and were asking to launch a program that's ran entirely by incarcerated individuals, where we design curriculum that is created by us and for us. After creating an executive board of men who understood the gang culture, who had respect in the prison community, and most importantly who had matured mentally while doing time, it was time to submit our proposal. A meeting was set with the wardens where we were allowed to pitch our idea, and in a short period of time we got the approval to move forward. Now all I had to do was go over policies, procedures, and create bylaws, while the guys who we now called community educators create their curriculum. This process would surely take some time.

I was faced with another major challenge. One day while I was at work, I received word that Akeem was involved in a gang fight and had been stabbed in the neck. For safety reasons, the entire prison was locked down. Akeem had managed to survive, but I would once again find myself battling with my post-traumatic street disorder mentality. The post-traumatic street disorder mentality was telling me that there was no way that I could let this go and that somebody had to pay for what happened to Akeem. But this new version of La'Ron that I had been working so hard to build was reminding me that I couldn't keep holding myself back in life on behalf of other people's problems, especially since the situation Akeem got involved in had nothing to do with him directly. And for Akeem and I there was never an issue about the situation; he respected that I was changing my life and even participated in the CAP months later.

While we were on lockdown for pending investigation, I sat in my cell battling with my thoughts and contemplating my next move. While doing so, I began to reflect on my past. I began to think about the day that Akeem approached me in high school about his problem with the Bloods, which resulted in me being expelled from school. I began to think about the time I had lost my sack, which resulted in a $5,600 loss. I began to think about all my friends who lost their lives. I even began to think about Milton and how his situation had nothing to do with me but I found myself involved in the altercation, which resulted in me doing life in prison. And this is not me saying that I blame them for how my life turned out, but this is me saying that I did some major self-reflection. I had to take a closer look at the choices I was making on behalf of other people that continued to affect my life in a negative way.

More importantly, I began to think about the sound of my loved one's voices on how they wanted or couldn't wait for me to be home. I began to think about all the incarcerated individuals/gang members behind the wall that looked toward me as a guiding compass, a positive example of change, for hope. In that moment I made the decision that there was no turning back and that I must continue to stay true to myself and to my journey. In turn, this would be that last battle between La'Ron and Clown, the biggest challenge I faced since the night of March 7, 2014. I was now 100 percent sure about the man I wanted to be, moving forward. Essentially my introduction to being a gang member started with Akeem and ultimately ended with Akeem. And I soon found out how this was one of the best choices I have ever made.

Less than two weeks later, I was able to mark my name in the Nebraska history book. On August 12, 2020, I was asked by the Nebraska Department of Corrections Directors if I would be willing to go speak with a group of young men at the Nebraska Correctional Youth Facility. This would make me the first convicted lifer in the state of Nebraska that was allowed to leave an adult prison to be around youths under the age of eighteen. This moment meant so much to me because from the jump I realized that this move was so much bigger than me and that I could possibly open the door for other lifers to take the trip. But more importantly, that I had the chance to break a cycle of historical trauma in the lives of young men who were still maturing mentally.

Shortly after, in March 2021, I made history once again with a group of respected incarcerated individuals at NSP. We launched the first program in Nebraska prison's history ran entirely by incarcerated individuals—the amazing Community Awareness Program, also known as CAP. Ultimately, this provided those at NSP with a platform for individuals that have been able to successfully transform their lives, a space to share lessons learned and different skills acquired by curriculum they created through CAP. The focus was on all of those who were gang members or had been incarcerated before the age of twenty-five. On average, we had anywhere from fifty to one hundred participants each class.

Furthermore, in June 2021, I and eight other men were a part of yet another groundbreaking move. We were approved to live at the Nebraska Correctional Youth Facility as intentional peer supporters—another move that was the first in the Nebraska prison system history.

* * * * *

In closing, I would like to add that writing this book has truly been a privilege and an honor. I myself had read this book many times, and I would describe it as an "all-purpose cleaner" for those who wish to step into their manhood and purify their mindset from the post-traumatic street disorder mentality. There are so many effective valuable life lessons included inside. If this book is used for its intended purpose, it truly has the power to transform trauma into emotional intelligence and create a healing process through strategic, vulnerable book club conversations.

The fact remains that there are so many of our at-risk youth that are growing up right now experiencing some of the same or similar situations and/or emotions that I felt with no clear understanding on what true change looks like because they are trying to survive day by day living in unfortunate environmental circumstances. Oftentimes doing what we think is right or forming this idea that we had no other choice looks like making bad choices or condoning in illegal activities just to get by in life. But it's my belief that once we begin to open up about our experiences, emotions, and struggles, it can create an opportunity for us to be heard and supported, and not judged, or put in those situations of "We're damned if we do and damned if we don't."

This book is not a proclamation that I have all the answers, but what I do know is if we fail to try, then we automatically fail. What I will say is that I truly understand how trying to change a mentality you have adopted or been taught in your childhood is hard to do, but we must understand change is a process. And when you're out there living in the moment, we fail to evaluate our process. And of course your process might not look like mine, but having insight and understanding the power to have the ability, to look at yourself objectively (self-reflection) is where you begin to look back on your life and understand your pitfalls, how you were misled, and how sharing your lived experience on growth can be liberating for our next generation. #SANKOFA

* * * * *

My grandmother, Betty Spencer, always told me that "God works in mysterious ways." Yes, he does! As I mentioned in chapter 7, I recall on many occasions evaluating my life and not truly understanding why God had allowed me to experience so much adversity. My mom had me at thirteen. I was abandoned as a

child. My dad committed suicide when I was five months young. I grew up in a household where I felt I didn't belong. I lost nine close friends to gun violence in a matter of three years. I also lost four other associates who weren't hood-affiliated to gun violence. I managed to survive being shot five times, which all happened on separate occasions. I have been betrayed by my closest friend(s). I have been harassed by the police, been falsely arrested for murder, spent eight months in jail before I was released. Now, I am doing life in prison and, may I add, sober. I also recall at trial, I asked those in the courtroom to pray for me. "Pray that this time makes me better and not bitter." Now when I begin to look at my life today and the many men that I have inspired, impacted in a positive way with my testimony on my lived experience and ultimately with my story of transformation, I understand why God has answered so many of my prayers.

I wholeheartedly understand that I have lived a life that has caused a ripple effect in my community. For those whose lives I have impacted directly or indirectly, I want you to know from the bottom of my heart that I sincerely apologize. For those whose lives I impacted directly in March 2014, I have submitted an "Accountability Letter" to the Nebraska Department of Corrections, Accountability Letter Bank. To view this letter, please contact the Nebraska Department of Corrections Service.

The Importance of Educating Yourself while Incarcerated

Left to Right La'Ron, Bernard, Akeem.

Kingzton and I at NSP in 2017, at a Defy Venture (now known as Rise) Business pitch. My son got to see me in my cap and gown. Also, I was one of the top 5 winners. Out of sixty-seven people, my son witnessed me winning third place.

The Importance of Educating Yourself while Incarcerated

Testing of Your Faith

Count it all joy, my brother, when you meet trials of various kinds, for you know that the testing of your faith produces steadfastness. And let steadfastness have its full effect, that you may be blessed, lacking in nothing. If any of you lack wisdom, let him ask God, who gives generously to all without reproach, and it will be given. But let him ask in faith, with no doubting, for the one who doubts is like a wave of the sea that is driven and tossed by the wind, for that person must not suppose that he will receive anything from God; he is a double-minded man, unstable in all his ways.

Let the lowly brother boast in his exaltation, and the rich in his humiliation, because like a flower of the grass he will pass away. For the sun rises with its scorching heat and withers the grass; its flower falls, and its beauty perishes. So also will the rich man fade away in the midst of his pursuits.

Blessed is the man who remains steadfast under trial, for when he has stood the test he will receive the crown of life, which God has promised to those who love him. Let no one say when he is tempted, "I am being tempted by God," for God cannot be tempted with evil, and he himself tempts no one. But each person is tempted when he is lured and enticed by his own desire. Then desire when it has conceived gives birth to sin, and sin when it is fully grown brings forth death.

Do not be deceived, my beloved brothers. Every good gift and every perfect gift is from above, coming down from the Father of lights, with whom there is no variation or shadow due to change. Of his own will he brought us forth by the word of truth, that we should be a kind of firstfruits of his creatures. (James l:2–18)

REVIEW BOOK CLUB QUESTIONS.

QUESTIONS FOR BOOK CLUB

These series of personal and self-reflecting questions are a guide to help create uncomfortable conversations, and for book club purpose, these questions should be discussed after every chapter. This process should be in a safe space and, more importantly, as authentic as possible. These questions are not an attempt to diagnose anyone, but intended for individuals to be more open about their lived experience and allow them to narrate their story in a way that is healing and helpful. Copy and print questions if needed.

Chapter 1: Birth of La'Ron

In many ways our parents' relationships with their parents often reflect the relationship they have with their kids, morals, values, religion, politics, etc. Parents' relationship with their kids should be built on unconditional love, a gift that cannot be earned or bought. History has shown us parenting was considered the model of authority, but most parents no longer want to see themselves as authority figures, but rather equal, and use their role to validate their children's feelings or rather play the role of a cool, submitting parent. Either way, all children will still go through stages of rebellion which, in turn, allows children to discover their own identity. When this process goes wrong, children tend to grow up too fast, making choices that they don't understand could possibly affect their whole life.

What part in this chapter do you relate to the most and why?

Questions for Book Club

What do you know about the state of your parents' relationship at the time of your birth?

Do you know how old your parents were when they had you, and do you feel like that was too young?

Have your parents or grandparents ever been to prison? If so, how do you think that affects you?

Do you believe there is guilt when a teen has a baby? And if so, who is more weighed down by the guilt, the parent or the child?

In your family, who do you see as strong-minded, and what do you admire about that person?

Chapter 2: Parentless Child

Oftentimes kids grow up in a household with one parent/guardian. Oftentimes this will lead to the guardian being overworked and figuring out other means to provide for their child/family. Being overworked, being a single parent, and being financially responsible, most guardians are plagued by the feeling of not building better relationships with their kids and feeling helpless which is often created by living paycheck to paycheck, by being the sole provider, and by many other personal and household stressors. Also, in other cases, there are guardians who suffer with mental illness and/or addiction and don't work and depend on state benefits, which in turn puts a child(s) in position of having to figure out how to raise and provide for themselves and/or siblings at a young age.

What part in this chapter do you relate to the most and why?

Questions for Book Club

Who raised you growing up?

_____

_____

_____

Have you ever lost a parent/guardian? If so, how did that make you feel?

_____

_____

_____

Did anyone in your household have mental illness problem or a drug addiction? If so, how do you think it affected your choices growing up?

_____

_____

_____

If you weren't raised by your parents but were raised by immediate family members, do you think they felt responsible to take you in?

_____

_____

_____

Would you condone an illegal activity to provide for your family? If so, why?

_____

_____

_____

Chapter 3: Childhood Trauma

Once again, for many of us there is so much we don't remember about our childhood, but I am sure growing up you were told a few stories about your upbringing. Trauma begins when you become more aware of what is going on around you that has a negative impact on your life, and that trauma can often shape how you view similar situations or the world around you forever. Of course, one lived experience could affect two people in different ways. I did my best in this chapter to shine light on a few situations that could change a person's worldview. I started this chapter on friendships and bullying, followed by relationship bonds, abandonment issues, and intentionally ended with a conversation that is taboo to many: being sexually violated. Writing this part of the book was one of the hardest stories to narrate, especially with the ending being false (chapter 4) and knowing that this is the sad reality for so many individuals which has caused a widespread of unnecessary trauma. Feel free to visit with your group facilitator for one-on-one conversation.

What part in this chapter do you relate to the most and why?

_____

_____

_____

Questions for Book Club

What is your earliest negative childhood memory, and how do you think this affects you today?

_____

_____

_____

If you didn't have a mother or a father in your life, do you think it would have made a difference. If so, how?

_____

_____

_____

What was some of your first memories of grade school?

_____

_____

_____

Have you ever had to take up for a friend who was being bullied? If so, what was that experience like?

_____

_____

_____

Have you ever been in trouble for something you didn't understand was wrong? If so, what was that experience like?

_____

_____

_____

Have you ever experienced bullying? If so, what were some of the emotions you felt?

_____

_____

_____

What was your first fight about?

_____

_____

_____

Did you ever have good relationships with your siblings? If not, why?

_____

_____

_____

Questions for Book Club

What activity did you enjoy most growing up and why?

_____

_____

_____

Chapter 4: Exposure

Exposure begins when we begin to understand life is more than what we see in our household. As the saying goes, "There is a whole other world on the other side of town." This is the moment when we become more curious, and without the proper guidance/influence, that curiosity can subject us to listen to the wrong storytellers. Oftentimes when there's no love or a listening ear in the household, kids will search for it in the streets. I believe it's safe to say, in most impoverished communities there is a culture of vultures that preys on the young mind in order to feed their own pride, ego, and self-worth, and these are the very people whose actions we end up imitating, because oftentimes the information they feed our young brain makes perfect sense to a person who has no answer to life's challenges. But as you read, there is a powerful message behind this chapter: be careful giving out hypocritical advice.

What part in this chapter do you relate to the most and why?

_____

_____

_____

Was there ever a time you felt that you had something important to talk about but you didn't feel comfortable discussing it with someone in your household? If so, who did you talk to, and what type of advice did you receive?

_____

_____

_____

Can you look back and remember a time you were misled? Now that you think about it, how does that make you feel?

_____

_____

_____

Have you ever run away from home? If so, what was that experience like for you?

_____

_____

_____

Growing up, how did you manage to deal with your anger, and what are some things you could have done differently?

_____

_____

_____

Questions for Book Club

What is the best advice you have been given, and why do you feel like it was great advice?

_____

_____

_____

What is something in your life that keeps you balanced? Explain why.

_____

_____

_____

What was something that you were exposed to that changed the direction of your life?

_____

_____

_____

Chapter 5: The Transition

As I mentioned before, no one was born to live a life of crime; something happens to you along the way. If we were all to look closely at our lives and ask where did we go wrong, I would almost guarantee that it has something to do with a transition in your life—state to state, changing houses, switching schools, new guardians, etc. For most gang members, I would say this transition may have happened for you in your neighborhood or in your school, anywhere

between fifth and ninth grade. Oftentimes these transitions lead to us searching for acceptance and our identity in the wrong places, and for some, the streets begin calling their name.

What part in this chapter do you relate to the most and why?

_____

_____

_____

What transition took place in your life when you noticed yourself getting off track?

_____

_____

_____

Who were some of your close friends, and what were all of your friendship like?

_____

_____

_____

What was the community/neighborhood like where you grew up in?

_____

_____

Do you think your environment played a part in how you grew up?

Name a time you found yourself searching for your identity and acceptance, and who did you try to imitate?

The first time you became aware of breaking the law, how did it make you feel? And was it because of financial reasons or because you were influenced to do so?

Have you ever been a part of a school click, and what was that experience like for you?

What was your greatest quality as a teen?

_____

_____

_____

Chapter 6: The Birth of Clown

This is the part of our lives where we begin to lose our identity and some of our core values that we were raised to believe. We begin to view much of ourselves and the world off what our culture creates. The image of our selves is based not on what is inside us but what is on or around us—the clothes we wear, how others see us, to overall becoming a product of our environment, etc. When it comes to the direct cause of us being influenced, we all have a story.

What part in this chapter do you relate to the most and why?

_____

_____

_____

Who was the first person you would say had a negative influence over your life and how?

_____

_____

_____

Questions for Book Club

What changed in how you viewed yourself at this time?

_____

_____

_____

What changed in how you viewed your environment at this time?

_____

_____

_____

What values were you raised on that you feel you started to stand less on, and what was the new thought that caused it?

_____

_____

_____

Have you ever been involved in a gang fight? If so, what was that experience like?

_____

_____

_____

Have you ever been suspended or expelled from school? If so, what was that experience like. And now that you look back, in what ways did getting suspended/expelled affected you negatively?

_____

_____

_____

What was one of the hardest conversations you had to have with your parents/guardian, and why was this conversation so hard to have?

_____

_____

_____

What was your experience like the first time you got in trouble with the law?

_____

_____

_____

Have you ever sold an immediate family member drugs, and what was your mindset behind doing so?

_____

_____

Have you ever felt like you were hustling backward? If so, explain why.

_____

_____

_____

Chapter 7: Post-Traumatic Street Disorder

This chapter gets away from the image of who or what we think we are and focuses on the mentality that forms when it relates to traumatic experience. There are many people around the world who were born with genetic mental illness, but there are also those whose mentality has been shifted by their environment/experiences. A few ills created from the streets are identity issues, social ills, fears, paranoia, trust issues, depression, addiction, and even worse, how we begin to view other people. For me, I began to look at these ills from a street-disorder perspective. I paid less attention to how we act and focused more on the cause and the mentality that makes us react.

What part in this chapter do you relate to the most and why?

_____

_____

_____

What was one of your biggest fears as you shifted more toward living a street life? In what ways did these fears affect your day-to-day living?

_____

_____

_____

What experience in your life had the worst effect on you and why?

_____

_____

_____

Did you often feel the only way to protect your family was to be around them less? Explain.

_____

_____

_____

Have you ever had someone close to you turn into your enemy? If so, how did that change your perspective on friendship?

_____

_____

_____

Questions for Book Club

Have you ever blamed God for your problems? And if so, why?

_____

_____

_____

Do you think it's hard to get money and gangbang at the same time? Why or why not?

_____

_____

_____

Have you ever been played out of your money? And if so, what was that experience like for you?

_____

_____

_____

What was your experience like the first time you were incarcerated?

_____

_____

_____

If you ever lost a close friend to gun violence, how did that make you feel and how did you process your emotions?

_____

_____

_____

Was there a person in your life that you felt like you could count on? And if so, what made this person so trustworthy?

_____

_____

_____

What does changing your life look like, and what would it take to do so?

_____

_____

_____

How do you cope with stressful situations?

_____

_____

_____

Questions for Book Club

Chapter 8: Warning Signs

When we were kids, I believe the first most common lesson we learn is the lesson of what's right and what's wrong. But just because we know it's wrong, that doesn't mean we will continue to make the right choices. Often in this book I spoke about the battle between La'Ron and Clown, and from my experience, when you have a desire to do and be better, your conscious has a way of talking to you through situations in life.

What part in this chapter do you relate to the most and why?

_____

_____

_____

Have you ever experienced warning signs in your life? And if so, what do you think were those warnings trying to show/tell you?

_____

_____

_____

Do you feel like there is or was a battle between good and evil in your life? Explain.

_____

_____

_____

Is there an omen in your life? If so, explain.

_____

_____

_____

What is a fear you have adopted from living the street life?

_____

_____

_____

What aspect of your life stopped you from being a better parent?

_____

_____

_____

Have you ever had a situation where you felt your lawyer violated your rights?

_____

_____

_____

Questions for Book Club

Chapter 9: The Fear of Death

This chapter is a direct connection to chapter 7, which tells that our street experience can create a negative mentality. In this chapter I highlighted my desire to change and the multiple reasons why I failed to do so. I once watched a documentary by Van Jones produced by CNN on a guy in California prison who killed a man's daughter. The victim's father went back into prison to look at his daughter's killer in the face, to ask why, and ultimately to forgive him. Looking at it from a restorative justice view, one of the guys made a statement that I will continue to remind others: "The worst thing about fear is what it does to you when we try to hide it." I often pondered on that statement, and now looking back, I can say that I hid my fears by buying materialistic items to make me feel good about my self-worth, drinking liquor to cope with my emotions, and continuing to lie to myself by putting a firearm on my hip and telling myself this was the only way I could stay alive.

What part in this chapter do you relate to the most and why?

_____

_____

_____

What part of your mindset was hard to change due to your past?

_____

_____

_____

Do you think staying out of your neighborhood could have assisted your personal change?

_____

_____

_____

In what ways have you felt like you couldn't win for losing?

_____

_____

_____

Have you ever felt like problems had a way of finding you? Explain.

_____

_____

_____

What issues do you feel like were the root of your life problems?

_____

_____

_____

Have you ever been harassed by the police, and what was that experience like for you?

_____

_____

_____

What was the biggest fear that you dealt with as a teen?

_____

_____

_____

Chapter 10: State of Nebraska Versus Jones

This chapter focuses on my case, my due process, my incarceration, and phases of emotions that I went through. This chapter also highlights a few issues in minor detail that I believe is an issue for those who are gang-affiliated and find themselves up against the justice system. Let me just say I get the whole idea behind being tough on crime, but is that personal or justice?

What part in this chapter do you relate to the most and why?

_____

_____

_____

Have you ever felt like God or Satan spoke to you?

_____

_____

_____

Have you ever witnessed your parent/guardian being abused by their mate? And if so, how did that make you feel?

_____

_____

_____

Do you think there are different values from the street life and family life? Explain.

_____

_____

_____

Have people you loved disappeared while you were doing time? And if so, how did you manage those emotions?

_____

_____

_____

Questions for Book Club

Have you ever felt like the justice system was against you? And if so, explain why.

_____

_____

_____

Have you ever been in a situation where you felt like you're damned if you do and you're damned if you don't?

_____

_____

_____

Chapter 11: The Importance of Educating Yourself While Incarcerated

I guess some may ask, why write about the importance of educating yourself while incarcerated in a book that's designed for youths? My answer is simple: it's about awareness. In 2021, Nebraska prison's incarceration rate was nearly 50 percent, higher than the United States Black rate. Black people make up about 5 percent of Nebraska's population, but 27 percent of the state incarcerated individuals. And on a larger scale, you have 2.3 million individuals incarcerated across the United States, and that's not counting the number of those who are on parole, probation, house arrest, etc. Oftentimes, in the gang culture, going to prison can be looked at as a way to earn stripes depending on your crime, which leads us to a sad reality. Many young women and men will find themselves doing time in somebody's jail or prison, and once you do, I believe it's very important for you to begin to educate yourself. This process shall include examining your mentality, thoughts, and emotions. Also the behavior that

led you to be in prison. One of the most valuable lessons I've learned from lifer in prison is, people do change; some of us just needed time to heal. I know I did!

What part in this chapter do you relate to the most and why?

_____

_____

_____

What does La'Ron mean by "The biggest barrier to wisdom is being judgmental?"

_____

_____

_____

How do you feel about gang members who have stepped away from the gang life?

_____

_____

_____

What do you think adults don't understand about the life that so many of us live in the streets?

_____

_____

Questions for Book Club

What do you think we, as a community, can do to prevent gun violence?

What do you value more, integrity or death before dishonor? Explain why.

What do you value more, real man or real n*gga? Explain why.

What do you value more, community or hood? Explain why.

What do you value more, family or homies? Explain why.

_____

_____

_____

Once you take away the gang life, the homies, the weapons, what do you stand for as an individual? Who are you?

_____

_____

_____

Connect to more resources by e-mailing ptsdvol1@gmail.com. Correspondence can be mailed to Post-Traumatic Street Disorder P.O. Box 24358, Omaha, Nebraska, 68124.